# BOOMERANG
# KIDS

# BOOMERANG KIDS

## How to Live with Adult Children Who Return Home

BY
### JEAN DAVIES OKIMOTO
AND
### PHYLLIS JACKSON STEGALL

LITTLE, BROWN AND COMPANY
BOSTON        TORONTO

FIRST EDITION


Excerpts from *The Prophet* by Kahlil Gibran reprinted by permission
of Alfred A. Knopf, Inc. Copyright 1923 by Kahlil Gibran and renewed 1951
by Administrators C.T.A. of Kahlil Gibran Estate, and Mary G. Gibran.


For reasons of privacy, the names
in this book have been changed.

*Library of Congress Cataloging-in-Publication Data*
Okimoto, Jean Davies.
    Boomerang kids.

    Bibliography: p.
        1. Adult children — United States — Psychology.
    2. Parents — United States.    I. Stegall, Phyllis Jackson.
    II. Title.
HQ799.97.U5055    1987        306.8'74        87-3274
ISBN 0-316-63810-2

RRD-VA

*Published simultaneously in Canada
by Little, Brown & Company (Canada) Limited*

PRINTED IN THE UNITED STATES OF AMERICA

10   9   8   7   6   5   4

To my daughter Amy

J.D.O.


To Sam and Anne, who gave me life;
To Margaret, Scott, Stephen, and Bill,
  who forgive me continually; and
To Fred, who enriches the adventures of my life

P.J.S.

# Contents

# Acknowledgments

WE ARE GRATEFUL to Ruth Cohen, our agent, who backed up her enthusiasm for the idea of *Boomerang Kids* by guiding and assisting us in the development of the original proposal, and continued with her warm encouragement and support throughout the project; to Melanie Kroupa and Amy Meeker for their editorial help; to Norman H. Davies, who generously provided statistical research for much of the material in the introduction; and to Drs. Joseph T. Okimoto and H. Frederick Stegall, who served as rich resources and constant objects.

# BOOMERANG KIDS

# Introduction

# Why Can't Johnny or Jane Leave?

## *What's Behind the Young Adult's Prolonged Dependence on the Family*

"WHAT'S WRONG WITH MY SON? Why can't he leave home? Sometimes it's hard to believe he's almost twenty-six. When I think back on where I was at his age, it's like night and day. I had a wife and two kids, and we had just bought our first house. Johnny can't even manage to make it in an apartment. *What's happened?*"

Like this father, parents all over the country are finding themselves baffled when they compare where they were in their young adult years with where many of their children are now. So many young adults have a prolonged period of dependence on their parents that Bill Cosby spelled out his concerns about it in a commencement address to University of South Carolina graduates in the spring of 1986. "All across this great nation," Cosby said, "people are graduating and going forth. My concern is whether they know where 'forth' is. The road home is already paved. 'Forth' is not back home. We love you and we are proud of you, and we are not tired of you . . . but we could get tired of you. 'Forth' could be next door to us, but you pay the rent."

As psychotherapists, we first noticed what seemed to be

a change in American family life in the early eighties as a growing number of parents began asking for help with problems caused by the return home of an adult child. Parents with varied circumstances — single parents, stepparents, and parents in long-term first marriages — were saying the same thing: *Help! What do we do now? How do we make this work?* All were intent on reducing the tensions of living with their adult children.

We heard from parents such as Vickie and Don, who had just celebrated their twenty-fifth wedding anniversary and were relishing their empty nest when their twenty-three-year-old daughter lost her job and returned home; stepparents such as Marcia, who, childless herself, found herself with a twenty-five-year-old stepson coming to live after he dropped out of graduate school; and single parents such as Barbara, who was just beginning to adjust to single life and enjoy her independence when her twenty-four-year-old daughter was divorced and returned home. Many of the parents we saw had elderly parents themselves; they felt trapped in the middle trying to meet the needs of two generations. The caretaker roles they had assumed had become so burdensome that they were finding it difficult to cope.

Almost everywhere we turned, we bumped into people who had young adult children boomeranging back home: friends, neighbors, colleagues, our own families. Then we began to notice newspaper articles on the phenomenon. It became clear that millions of middle-aged parents in the mid-eighties were finding themselves nursing returned grown children through broken romances, lost jobs, and financial slumps.

The resulting confusion seemed to be growing as fast as the incidence of the phenomenon itself, creating a need for practical, positive solutions that were clear and precise. How could a parent show care and support for the adult child without returning to parent-child roles of earlier years? How could one best help the young adult with an emotional setback? How does one set limits and share physical and psychological territory? How does one understand and accept feelings of anger and resentment? There must be a way to avoid the predictable pitfalls of former parent-child roles and find a more mature and satisfying adult-to-adult relationship with these grown children.

To respond to this need, we set out to study the ways different families have handled the return home of an adult child (aged eighteen to twenty-nine). We knew many such families in Seattle; hoping for a broader base, we found families in Boston, San Diego, Houston, El Paso, Baltimore, Berkeley, Chicago, Boulder, Salt Lake City, and New York who shared with us their experiences with their own boomerang kids. We have changed names and any identifying information, but the feelings represented, the difficulties and conflicts experienced, and the solutions or lack of them are authentic, typical, and revealing. Most of the families we talked with could readily think of dozens of examples of friends and relatives who also were living with adult children, and it became increasingly clear to us that the phenomenon of delayed independence represented a true change in American family life.

## Delayed Independence

Let's look at the phenomenon of delayed independence itself. According to family demographers at the U.S. Census Bureau, 22 million young adults are now sharing the same household as their parents, almost a 50 percent increase since 1970. And in 1984, over *half* (52 percent, to be exact) of all young men aged twenty to twenty-four were living at home. The facts and trends are as clear as the numbers collected for the census over the years. Today's under-thirty generation is staying home longer than any generation since the first years after World War II. Why? How are things different?

## The Sexual Revolution and Later Marriages

The parents of boomerang kids tended to establish their own households not long after they reached the age of twenty. Reaching their majority in the fifties and early sixties, they were neither fish nor fowl, a generation on the cusp between two very different eras. They were adolescents in the fifties, when sexual mores were extremely conservative by today's standards. At that time there was only one societal standard regarding sexuality: premarital sex is immoral. As Frank Conroy wrote in describing sex and the fifties generation, "Needless to say, we lived and breathed hypocrisy."[1] They also married young. Coed college dorms and cohabitation, or POSSLQ's (people of the opposite sex sharing living quarters), as the census calls it, didn't exist. The only way to have sex without guilt and hypocrisy was to marry, and marry they did. In 1960, 72 percent of women between the ages of twenty and twenty-four were married. In 1984 only 43 percent of women in that age group were married. There has been almost a 50 percent drop in the marriage rate of young adults compared to their parents' generation. And among Americans aged thirty to thirty-five, the percentage of people who have never married has doubled since 1970.

Later marriages are the result of a radical change in attitudes since the late fifties. When this change first appeared in the early sixties, it was labeled "the new morality." In 1962 a national magazine polled college students on attitudes toward premarital sex and reported that nearly all respondents, male and female, said that "sexual behavior is something you have to decide by yourself."[2] Things had changed radically, from "Premarital sex is immoral" to "It's up to you."

This change in the moral code was later to be called the sexual revolution and was strongly influenced by a new contraceptive–the pill. Since the sexual revolution of the sixties, young adults have been going to bed, and not as often to the altar. In spite of the Moral Majority and the resurgence of conservative religious thinking in the early part of this decade, living with someone without being married is not considered by many people today to be living in sin. It's just one way a lot of people live.

## The Rise in Divorce

The changes in social customs have also been reflected in the divorce rate, which has doubled since 1970. In 1983 there were over half a million divorced people aged twenty to twenty-four. Although there are no statistics available on how often unmarried couples who have been living together break up, we can speculate that the rate approximates that of divorce, and probably exceeds it. Where do young adults go when their marriage or their relationship ends? Often they go home. In this way they differ from their parents' generation. The last thing a sixties young adult wanted to do if things weren't going well was go home to Mother. The generation gap was just too big. Mother would never have understood the new morality. The idea of living at home seemed so oppressive that it was out of the question. But today the generation gap has narrowed, so young adults can go home to parents who are sociologically and psychologically closer to their children than any previous generation.

The parents of today's young adults were themselves young adults when the pill was invented. Their attitudes about sex are closer to their children's than to their own parents'. They were the first generation to love Elvis; they rocked around the clock to Bill Haley and the Comets; and their jitterbugging was soon followed by some shake, rattle, and rolling. They were the first generation of rock. Many of the voices they loved when they were young adults are still around: Bob Dylan, Diana Ross, and Ray Charles, to name just a few, have created whole arenas of pop music today where these two generations overlap.

The parents of today's young adults were also the generation that began the spiraling divorce rate in the seventies; they've shared with their children the pain of broken families. Today's young adults, if they were children of divorce, inevitably had some very difficult and unstable childhood years. This may contribute to making it harder for many of them to grow up.

In fact, parents' divorce often plays a major role in the delayed separation of their children. Dad and Mother may have unfinished business about the ending of their marriage, and often much of this is guilt about what the breakup of the family did to the children involved. They know they've hurt their kids by getting divorced, and when the children who are now adults want to come home, they try to make up for all the hurt by taking them in with no expectations and no questions asked.

## Lack of Role Models and Rites of Passage

Many parents just don't know how to let go of their children. Their own parents may not have been good role models for this, and as young adults themselves they may have had to struggle to get free. When they were young adults, however, it was more common for young women to marry just to get away from home, or for young men to go into the army for the same reason, and thus their parents were forced to surrender their place of authority;

they were forced to see their daughter as a married woman or their son as a soldier, making it harder to continue to treat them as children who needed their care. Marriage and the military were traditional rites of passage.

Since December of 1974, however, an all-volunteer army has resulted in fewer numbers of men aged twenty to twenty-four in the military. According to Department of Defense figures, since 1970 there has been a 40 percent drop in the rate at which people enter the military. Without this traditional avenue of independence, which forced responsibility, young men in this age group are having a hard time growing up and becoming independent. More than half of them continue to live at home. Without the usual rites of passage such as marriage or the military providing that natural step away from home, neither parents nor their young adult children have an easy time shifting from parent-child ties to adult-to-adult roles.

## The Economy

When the parents of boomerang kids got married in the late fifties and early sixties, the common American dream was a house in the suburbs with two children, a dog, and a station wagon. The kids were supposed to grow up, leave home, and go to college. Then they were supposed to get a good job and get married. They *weren't* supposed to come back home.

But just as those kids were on the verge of becoming adults, the economy changed dramatically. The cost of living has increased by 267 percent since 1970. College costs have skyrocketed, from $1,051 for tuition and room and board at a state university in 1965 to $3,670 in 1985. Private college tuition and room and board fees have increased by at least four times since 1965. The undergraduate tuition and room and board fees for the 1986–87 school year in ten leading private universities (MIT, Harvard, Yale, Dartmouth, Princeton, Brown, Columbia, Stanford, University of Pennsylvania, Northwestern) range from $15,103 to $16,296. Many families and kids themselves have had to sacrifice and work hard to pay for school expenses. Often a young adult attends college for a while, drops out to work and save money, then returns again to complete college. The result is a prolonged college education and a prolonged period of dependence on the family.

But the carrot on the other end of all this expensive education isn't always that "good" job that provides a reasonably comfortable life-style. Entry-level salaries have not kept up with entry-level housing costs.

Although median earnings have increased almost two and a half times since 1970, the purchasing power of the dollar has fallen by almost 300 percent. Early in 1986, in an article on the economy, Texas congressman Jim Wright wrote:

> The beer commercial "you can have it all" sounds a kind of anthem for America's young, prosperous, upwardly mobile professionals who are supposed to typify their generation. Unfortunately, the myth hides an ugly fact. Most of America's young adults are not upwardly mobile. For as long as anyone can remember, the heart of the American experience has been upward mobility. What we now see is something alien and unacceptable: a downward mobility, a slippage in living standards from parents to children. Today a thirty-year-old male head of household earns about 10 percent less in real buying power than his father did at the same age. In the 1950s, a 30-year-old man earned about one-third more than his father had at the same stage in life.

For baby-boomers of average income, the so-called

recovery has been something of a bust. Most 25- to 40-year olds find it harder than their parents did to own a home, to save any money, or to send their children to college. One big reason is the doubling of home prices since 1970. In that year, three of every four Americans could afford to buy an average-priced house. By 1984, only one in three could do so. Projections suggest that, in the absence of a dramatic change in direction, fewer than one-half of all Americans under the age of 30 will ever enjoy the privilege of owning a home. . . . A family that spends nearly half of its income on mortgage payments has far too little left to pursue other aspects of the American dream such as education, leisure, or savings.[3]

## Young Adults Strapped Financially

These young adults have more problems than not being able to save for education and leisure time. Not only have their entry-level salaries not kept up with inflation, but many have had trouble finding jobs at all. Since 1979 nearly 2 million manufacturing jobs have disappeared; the unemployment rate, now at 6.9 percent, has remained higher than during any previous postwar recovery. In addition, rent on the same apartment has doubled since 1970, while food costs have doubled and in some areas tripled. Young people starting out on their own have been landing in poverty at alarming rates. Among persons under twenty-five with their own households, 33 percent lived in poverty in 1984, up from 20 percent in 1979.[4]

For many young adults, the only solution was shared housing. In unprecedented numbers they formed households with other young adults. But finding compatible roommates didn't always happen easily on the first try, and many shared housing situations fell apart. What to do until they could find a better housing situation? Move back home, of course.

## The Designer Life-style

Not only did many young adults living on their own find their housing situations less than desirable, but they missed the middle-class life-style they had when they lived with their parents. The young adults of today have spent many formative and impressionable years in a society that worshiped "the right stuff," not the stuff of character, but things, things, and more things: the right label, the right brand, the right make, the right model, the right name, *the right stuff*. Consumerism and materialism have caused many young adults to covet a designer life-style. A recent Gallup survey of college freshmen found that the percentage who think it is essential or very important to be "very well off financially" has jumped from 43.5 percent in 1967 to almost 70 percent today. A Forbes survey of students aged eighteen to twenty-two found that "almost 78% feel that choosing a low paying field that you like is a mistake . . . only 37% felt that way in 1966."[5] But the lifestyle they covet is one they can't easily afford on their own. There has been pressure to climb fast and acquire much, a pressure that gives rise to unrealistic expectations on the part of young adults whose paychecks will not support their upwardly mobile tastes — unless they move home.

With joblessness at an all-time high since the depression, and salaries not keeping up with inflation, parents of today's young adults no longer automatically believe that their children's lives will be better than their own. In fact, they fear their children's lives may be a lot worse. They want their children to be financially secure and are willing to prolong their dependence, thinking they can help them get that security. They let them come home to save money.

## Alcohol, Drug Abuse, and Emotional Problems

Not all boomerang kids come home because of losing a job, financial trouble, dropping out of school, the end of a relationship, or wanting to save money. Some come home because of emotional problems that led to alcohol and drug problems. Cocaine abuse is the fastest-growing drug problem in America; its debilitating effects often send young adults back to their parents. They land on the doorstep emaciated, depressed, and penniless. According to estimates by the National Institute on Drug Abuse, reported in *Newsweek,* cocaine users increased from 15 million to 22 million between 1979 and 1982. The problem is most prevalent among young adults.

The suicide rate among young adults continues to climb as well. According to the *Harvard Medical School Mental Health Letter,* suicide is the tenth leading cause of death in the United States, with nearly 30,000 suicides reported annually. The suicide rate for ages fifteen to twenty-four has risen 150 percent in the last twenty years. This age group, which in 1965 accounted for 5 percent of all suicides, now accounts for 20 percent of male and 14 percent of female suicides.[6]

We found that whether adult children returned home because of emotional problems, a drug or alcohol problem, losing a job, financial trouble, dropping out of school, the end of a relationship, or wanting to save money, their families were faced with many of the same problems of daily living. Part of the title of *Boomerang Kids* is "How to Live with Adult Children Who Return Home," but in the broadest context our book is about separation. It is about helping young adults develop the capacity to leave you and make it on their own.

# ONE

---

# Guess Who's Coming to Dinner?

## *What Happens to the Family When the Adult Child Returns Home*

---

GUESS WHO'S COMING TO DINNER — and for breakfast and lunch and to spend the night, and the week . . . and months . . . and . . . ?

Parents often find it upsetting when their adult child leaves home but then, like a boomerang, comes sailing back. Expecting that their children at eighteen or twenty-one will be ready to go out into the world as capable, independent people who can do whatever it takes to run their own lives, many parents believe that at that magic moment their role as parents will be over. Where did so many of us get the idea that fully functioning adulthood occurs at age eighteen? In reality, adult children often try their wings, fall on their faces, and return home to regroup, recoup, and eventually try again. People, like flowers, bloom at different rates, and some young adults take longer to mature than others.

Children have tasks to master at each stage of their growth. For instance, the one-year-old must learn to walk, the two-year-old must learn to talk. The one-year-old will fall quite a few times before he or she perfects the art of walking, and the two-year-old mispronounces all kinds of words before mastering language. Young adults, just like those toddlers who fall down and get back up again repeatedly, may have to try more than once to leave the nest, stumbling on their way to full independence. As parents, we're apt to have difficulty understanding that the developmental task of late adolescence and young adulthood, that of separating from us as parents, is, in fact, an ongoing process.

Some parents feel that an adult child who needs to return home is a failure. In thinking that the child is a failure, they feel that they too have failed. This is frequently just not the case. More often, the young adult has merely stumbled on the way to independence and needs to come home for some help before getting ready to try again. Try to avoid the use of the word *failure,* both in your thinking and in your communicating with your adult child. Dealing with the return home is difficult enough, with both sides already experiencing some less-than-positive feelings. Rather, try to look at your child's return within the larger framework of the young adult's entire development, and to accept that return as a new opportunity to rework and reconstruct the relationship, enabling the young person to achieve successful independence as soon as possible. As with many experiences in life, it's important to see this experience as a problem to be solved, and to begin immediately to look at ways both generations can find solutions. In most cases, it is helpful to remember that the return home is a temporary one because the young adult has only been *temporarily* unsuccessful at independently leading his or her own life. Just because the first flight out of the nest was difficult doesn't mean the next one will be.

The adjustment to this life change will vary from family to family, but it helps to stay focused on the end point of what the young adult is striving for: the attainment of full independence.

Tom and Ann, both fifty-one years old, of Baltimore, Maryland, experienced many of the problems common to parents when a young adult moves back in. They had always had a happy marriage. But now in their middle years, with their kids grown and gone, they had rediscovered each other and enjoyed life in a new way. Their two children were living out-of-state. Dave, twenty-seven, a stockbroker in Atlanta, was married to a young woman whom Tom and Ann both liked. Susan, twenty-four, a legal assistant in Washington, D.C., was living with Bob, a lawyer who worked in the same firm.

Tom and Ann would have preferred to see Susan married to Bob rather than living with him, but they accepted the arrangement. Every few months they flew to Atlanta to see Dave or drove into Washington to have dinner with Susan — but they never really missed their kids. They loved their empty nest and being simply a couple again. Tom liked to tell his favorite joke about when life begins: "A priest, a minister, and a rabbi were having a discussion about when life begins. The priest said it began at conception, the minister said at birth, and the rabbi said, 'Life begins when the kids leave home and the dog dies.' "

Ann told a close friend that she was reexperiencing the excitement she felt when they were first married, and she sometimes overheard Tom refer to her as his "bride." Their circle of friends called them "the perfect couple."

Tom was a sales manager for a medical supply company. Ann had gone back to work when Susan finished high school, and still enjoyed her work as a French teacher. Spending weekends browsing around antique shops, they excitedly found pieces of furniture to add to the household, turning one of the kids' bedrooms into the Early American guest room Ann had always longed for and the other into a comfortable den for Tom. They enjoyed cooking creatively together in their newly remodeled kitchen and had a special dinner at home in the middle of each week. Their sexual relationship had never been better; when Susan first moved out, Tom said, "You know, Annie, we can make love in any room in the house."

It all changed abruptly one evening when Tom and Ann got a phone call from their daughter. At first Ann did not recognize Susan's voice because she was crying so hard. Susan explained that her relationship with Bob was over. On his thirtieth birthday the week before he had told Susan he no longer wanted to be "tied down." And then Susan sobbed, "Mom, I just want to come back home." Reassuring her daughter that she and Tom would do whatever they could to help, Ann said that of course she could plan to visit them. Susan explained that she wanted to come that evening since she refused to spend another night in the apartment she shared with Bob. Ann said they would wait up for her. When Ann relayed to Tom what had happened, he was furious with Bob.

Later that evening when Susan arrived, she added that she had also quit her job, unable to face Bob every day at work. She wanted to live at home for a while until she could get back on her feet, find another job, and figure out where to go from there. Although they both swallowed hard, Tom and Ann agreed that she could stay as long as she needed to.

Tom rented a truck and drove to Washington to help Susan bring home her furniture and belongings. Storing her things took up half the garage, so Tom began to park on the street.

In the weeks that followed, Susan was depressed and withdrawn. Her parents worried to themselves but tried not to make any demands. Susan took over the guest room, staying up late, turning up the sound on her stereo. After a month she still had not begun to look for a job. One morning, after a restless night for both Tom and Ann, Tom expressed his irritation that Susan never left the house. "Doesn't it bother you that we can't have an evening at home alone?" he asked his wife in an annoyed tone. Ann asked him to try to be more patient. "I miss you, too," she said, "but Susan really needs us now."

Secretly, Ann began to feel guilty, questioning her parenting of Susan, wondering how Susan's problem reflected on her as a mother. Tom's resentment grew, and he grumbled about parking on the street, hearing the phone ring so often for Susan, paying escalating grocery bills, seeing dirty dishes in the sink, having to nag about the stereo. He and Ann began to fight.

One evening, after Ann wondered out loud about what they might have done wrong, Tom exploded in fury: "Enough! She's twenty-four years old — not some lovesick teenager. I want my house back! I want my wife back!"

*What were Tom and Ann feeling?* Initially, their first response was to comfort Susan and empathize with her. Their child was hurt, and their instinct was to take care of her unconditionally. Ann reacted strongly to Susan's return home: "My child is in pain, and I must help her."

After their initial acceptance of Susan's need to move back in, they soon were confronting a loss on four different levels. The first loss was of their image of their daughter. They had considered her to be a competent, effectively functioning person. Now she was vulnerable and dependent, moody and uncooperative; and this evoked, in Ann particularly, a sense of guilt. "My child isn't performing well. I must have done something wrong." This second dimension of loss was a severe blow to Ann's self-esteem, to her self-image as a competent person and effective parent.

In addition to the increasing tension in dealing with their daughter, Tom and Ann had to accept a loss in their relationship. Before Susan's return home, they had been relating as a man and a woman; now they reverted to their roles as parents confronting a troubled child. Their reawakened sense of freedom and spontaneity disappeared, and the newly found intimacy they had treasured was disrupted.

The fourth loss was that of space or territory. The guest room and the garage were no longer theirs to use as they wished; in addition, their own psychological space was narrowed or diminished when their daughter inhabited their home.

*What went wrong?* Overwhelmed by their daughter's distress, Tom and Ann did not recognize what their adult child needed in this crisis; instead, they responded to Susan as if she were a small child. They allowed Susan to return home unconditionally. They did not discuss how long she would be living with them and what her role *as another adult* in the household would be. They failed to move from the position of immediate support when the crisis first occurred to one of requiring that she function as a contributing member of the household. In the process they ignored their own needs.

### What could they have done?

1. From the first moment Susan asked to return home, they could have answered, "Yes, of course you can come home, and after you take a day or two to settle in, we'll talk about where we go from here."

2. Tom and Ann could have talked with Susan about how long she would stay. After asking her "How long do you think you will need to live at home?" together, they could have agreed on a mutually acceptable period of time.

3. Tom and Ann could have discussed with Susan the impact on them of having another adult member of the

household. They could have said, "We've been used to having a lot of peace and quiet, and we like to keep things pretty orderly. While you're living here we want to be helpful to you and we expect that within reason you will adapt to our needs."

Tom and Ann needed to have adult expectations of Susan. They needed to have time alone, spending evenings out together to nurture their independence and privacy.

## Adult Expectations

One of the most important jobs parents have is to prepare their child for the world — and the world has expectations. What can parents rightfully ask of a young person who is turning to them for help? While each family has its own pattern, generally a young adult can be expected to take over a larger and larger share of responsibility for his or her world, which includes

1. Taking responsibility for self. This is a big umbrella for taking care of whatever the individual needs are: enough sleep, the right kind of food, appropriate clothing, adequate health care, safe transportation, getting places, keeping appointments.

2. Solving personal problems. Whatever isn't working, the young person is expected to take responsibility for his or her share of the problem, look at other options, and find solutions that get him or her back on track.

3. Being thoughtful of other people and responsive to their needs, whether the needs are for private time, shared but quiet time, companionship, equal use of the phone or car or television, neatness, or the like.

4. Committing to serious study and/or engaging in income-producing work. If the young adult is not in school, he or she is expected to find a job in order to share in

the costs of living with the parents as well as become financially independent as soon as possible.
5. Managing finances. Young people can reasonably be expected to unravel the mysteries of checkbooks, budgets, and saving for a rainy day.

These expectations seem obvious enough, and at first glance none of them is too much to expect of a young adult. They are the basic building blocks every young adult needs to construct his or her place in a larger society. However, these are the issues around which conflict is most apt to develop when the adult child returns home.

The loss of physical territory was the most stressful aspect in the relationship between Kristine, a forty-seven-year-old New York single parent, and her twenty-seven-year-old son, Jeff. Jeff's father, Bill, was a successful surgeon when he divorced Kristine. At thirty-seven she was left with three children, aged ten, twelve, and seventeen. The divorce was angry, painful, and bitter. Bill had had an affair with a young woman medical student during the last year of their marriage. After the divorce he married the young woman, started a second family, and now had four-year-old twins. Marrying right after she had finished college, Kristine had never held a job. The divorce settlement included generous child support, funds for the children's college education, three years of alimony, and money for Kristine to complete further education and become self-supporting.

She trained as a Montessori teacher and used some of the money she saved from her divorce settlement to establish a school. Her two daughters were both in expensive private colleges. Jeff had finished college, worked first in a bank, and then for an insurance company, and now was affiliated with a real estate firm as a commercial salesperson.

Kristine had fully recovered from the divorce and at last found herself enjoying life. She had a small one-bedroom condominium, and had begun dating a forty-nine-year-old aerospace engineer who lived in the same condominium complex.

Jeff received a salary from the real estate firm for a year and then straight commissions after that. When sales were few and far between, he began to have trouble meeting car payments and rent on his apartment. He and his father saw each other occasionally, and Bill had loaned money to his son several times after Jeff graduated from college. When the real estate market collapsed and Jeff ran out of money, he again turned to his father for help. This time Bill refused. "Look, I'm paying twenty-five thousand dollars a year for your sisters' colleges. I've already spent forty thousand dollars on your schooling, to say nothing of the arm and leg all those years of child support and your mother's education cost me. I'll be damned if I'll pay any of you another cent!"

The week Jeff's car was repossessed and he got an eviction notice, he moved in with his mother.

Kristine agreed to let Jeff stay with her until he found another job. She bought a sofa bed for the living room and put Jeff's belongings in storage. Most of Kristine's money was tied up in her school, so although she was comfortable, she was forced to live frugally.

Kristine felt the divorce had been hardest on Jeff, the oldest, and she remembered the effect her own devastation and depression had had on him at that time. What should have been carefree teenage years for him were instead years when he had felt caught between his parents and responsible for his mother. Jeff had been torn apart by Kristine's anger toward his father and her resentment of Bill's new wife. His immaturity and difficulties in managing his own life now, Kristine felt, resulted from that painful time. She feared that if she didn't let him stay with her his problems might develop into more serious trouble.

When Jeff moved in, Kristine was extremely supportive, but soon she found herself becoming increasingly resentful. The presence of a twenty-seven-year-old man in her small, well-organized space was intrusive. When she left for work, Jeff was still asleep, and when she returned the bed was still unmade. He borrowed her car to look for work, and when he picked her up, the gas tank was generally empty. As time went on, she grew irritated and impatient.

Worst of all, Kristine found herself reexperiencing the rage she had felt toward her former husband, fury she thought she had finished with years ago. Once again she blamed Bill for leaving her. She was envious of his financial situation and furious that he would not help Jeff. Kristine felt trapped and, as the tension mounted, more and more depressed. Her sense of having let Jeff down, her loss of self-esteem, and her increased financial strain were as intense for her as their similar feelings had been for Tom and Ann when their daughter returned home. But these were further complicated in Kristine's case by a terrible sense of guilt. She felt she had not parented Jeff adequately during the period before and after the divorce, and her responses to his return home now reflected this unresolved guilt. "Somehow I failed. Now I must make it up to him."

Kristine's feelings of guilt prevented her from effectively facing the problem of her present living situation and from focusing on what Jeff, as an adult child, needed from her. Like many people overwhelmed by such feelings, she felt unable to move on.

## Coping with Guilt and Anger

Guilt often immobilizes. Feeling guilty about the past keeps you from being able to see what is needed in the present.

Guilt associated with "unacceptable" feelings such as anger further complicates the picture because you then feel guilt about feeling angry — starting a cycle that is very hard to break.

Guilt is an internal process. Every grown-up who is mature psychologically has a conscience that contains his or her ideals, goals, and standards of what it means to be a human being. One of the ways this structure works is that people compare what they do and think and feel with these internal rules, and decide whether their actions or thoughts or feelings are acceptable or unacceptable. These rules can be healthy and realistic, or unhealthy and unrealistic. For example, an ideal of perfection is unrealistic. It can't be lived up to and often prevents people from taking any step that poses some risk. Striving to improve, on the other hand, can be a healthy part of one's internal code.

You feel guilty when you break your own code of what's right for you. You have let yourself down and, having disappointed yourself, you punish yourself with guilty feelings. Guilt is something you do to yourself.

In working through guilt you will need to root out its source. It is not a simple onetime process; self-acceptance often takes a lifetime of self-analysis. Start by asking yourself, "How have I let myself down? Which of my feelings, thoughts, and actions are unacceptable to me?" It can be helpful to write down whatever comes to mind without censoring your thoughts.

You might begin this task of accepting the past by telling yourself, "That happened. I cannot change one minute of the past." Forgiving yourself for the past is an important part of putting it to rest. Tell yourself, "I did the best I could then, given who I was, what I had, what I knew, who was involved, and what was possible." Isn't doing one's best, in fact, all you would expect of someone else? Each time you find yourself reviewing the past critically and with bad feelings, use such phrases to help yourself move forward to what's going on right now.

To keep yourself in the present, spend time answering such questions as "What do I *want* to provide for my adult child?" as distinguished from "What *should* I provide?" "Should" can be a trap: it's possible that some of what you feel you *should* provide really isn't appropriate or helpful for an adult child.

You may want to write these things down to help organize your thinking. Sharing your ideas with a friend who will likely be more objective than you are can also help you clarify your thinking. It's important to focus on "What are *my* needs?" in addition to "What are my adult child's needs?" Realistically assess where you are today by asking, "Given who I am, what I have, what can I realistically give to my adult child today?" Trying to do the impossible will inevitably lead to frustration, resentment, and anger.

Working through your anger is hard, but not impossible. Anger is a normal human response. It serves the defensive purpose of driving away someone who has hurt or threatened you in some way. You may be uncomfortable with your anger, seeing it as a weakness. Acceptance of anger begins with thinking about this feeling as part of your humanity. Remember that feelings are just feelings; as such, there are no "good" feelings or "bad" feelings. And feelings are not the same as actions. Your anger can be used as a signal to begin to sort out what's going on. It can help to give it some physical discharge, such as going for a brisk walk, or jogging, or pulling weeds, or playing a hard game of tennis. The action buys you time and gives you a chance to move from *feeling* to *thinking*. Acting while you are angry is often hurtful and unproductive, and usually interferes with successful problem-solving.

Feelings of helplessness contribute to and prolong anger. You can combat this by separating the things you can do something about from those over which you have no control. For example, you cannot change the fact that your adult child is in trouble right now and in need of help, but you *are* in charge of how much and what kind of help you offer. Sorting out what's possible from what isn't begins to move you out of the position of feeling stuck and allows you to see what you can do.

Kristine's situation would have had a different outcome had she been able to put the feelings of the past behind her and think about what she had to do in the present. Her guilt about the conflict and deprivation Jeff lived through during his adolescence was stopping her from doing what was best for him today. Her anger toward Jeff for interrupting her life was displaced onto her former husband for all his past mistakes, and she was unable to use her angry feelings appropriately to call a halt to Jeff's thoughtless and immature behavior.

Keep these things in mind as you work through the uncomfortable feelings of guilt and anger:

1. Stay in the present. Avoid endlessly reviewing the past.
2. Forgive yourself for what has happened and for not living up to your own standards.
3. Use your feelings as a signal that you need to take time to think about what's going on, and then use that time to become aware of what is stimulating your feelings, both in the past and in the present.
4. Make the changes you can, and work on accepting things that cannot be altered.
5. Pay attention to your own needs.

## Stepparents and Boomerang Kids

Guilt took a slightly different form when Stephanie decided to allow her stepdaughter Patti to move in. In this case, the returning young adult provoked a different dilemma.

Stephanie, thirty-six, was the only woman vice president of a Chicago bank. She had never had any desire to have children with her equally successful husband, Brian, forty-five, CEO of a large meat-packing company. Stephanie and Brian lived in a condominium on Chicago's Gold Coast along the shore of Lake Michigan. They had been married for five years and enjoyed a busy life. They infrequently saw Brian's two daughters from his first marriage, who had lived in Winnetka with their mother, and Stephanie had never resented Brian's child support and college tuition payments.

Stephanie and Brian had just returned from the Caribbean when Brian received a call from the emergency room at Cook County Hospital. His nineteen-year-old daughter, Patti, had overdosed on aspirin and alcohol.

When Brian met with the staff psychiatrist at the hospital, he learned that Patti, whose self-esteem was closely tied to her academic achievements, had been overwhelmed by college. She had struggled academically for the first time in her life and doubted her self-worth. Patti's mother, Brian's ex-wife, had just remarried and was on a honeymoon trip in Europe. Patti felt abandoned. She became increasingly depressed. Unable to sleep or eat, she fell behind in her classes, which added to her feelings of worthlessness. Her suicidal behavior was a cry for help.

After a two-week hospital stay, Patti was released to Brian and Stephanie's care. Brian, whose career had always come first, had never been much of a family man. He loved his daughters but had admitted to Stephanie that, although he felt uncomfortable about this, he was probably someone who never should have had children. When the psychiatrist told him that her mother's leaving on her honeymoon had caused Patti to reexperience the trauma of Brian's leaving the family when she was twelve, Brian became overwhelmed with guilt and determined to try to help her.

Stephanie felt she had no choice but to make the best of the situation, even though when she married Brian she had never bargained on having his children live with them. She felt guilty about not wanting Patti now. But she came home every night to make dinner for the three of them, let Patti borrow her clothes, and tried to adapt to the role of stepmother.

Patti was angry and demanding. Because of his guilt, Brian took all the verbal abuse Patti dished out. When Stephanie tried to talk to him about this, he became defensive. They argued bitterly and frequently. Stephanie developed severe headaches at work when five o'clock rolled around and it was time to go home. She confided in a coworker, "This is not what I signed up for!" For the first time she began to think about divorce.

Stephanie and Brian's marriage had never included any expectation or experience of parenting. When they were not responsible for anyone other than themselves, their marriage had worked. But their relationship could not tolerate the emotional demands of a young adult in crisis. Brian was unable to handle Stephanie's criticism of him or of Patti. Stephanie felt left out when Brian made it clear that Patti was his child and she didn't have anything to say about how he handled her.

Stephanie lost not only the privacy of her home but, unable to approach the problem with Brian as a partner, the closeness she had enjoyed with her husband.

The feelings with which parents struggle when an adult child returns home are often intensified for a stepparent. Gary and Margie, a boomerang stepfamily, had been married for eighteen years. At the time they married, they each had children from their previous first marriages. Margie had custody of her two sons, eight and five. Gary had a son and a daughter, seven and ten, who lived with their mother and visited him and Margie on weekends.

Gary, a successful accountant, paid almost twice as much child support over the years as Margie's ex-husband, a community college teacher, paid to her. Although Gary knew and understood that he paid more because he earned more, there were still times when he resented it. He and Margie both looked forward to the day when their child-raising obligations would be over, leaving them more income to keep for themselves and allowing them for the first time to have a relationship with each other that would not include children. When the last of the children graduated from high school, Margie and Gary found their new freedom every bit as gratifying as they had hoped.

Their time alone came to a halt when Margie's son Eric, twenty-three, ran into financial trouble his first year after college. He turned to Margie and Gary for help, asking to move back home to save money and pay off his bills. Gary, who had a good relationship with his stepson, didn't want to refuse to help him, but he deeply resented the fact that he had already provided the lion's share of the support not only for his own children, but for his stepchildren. The small amount of child support Eric's father had paid ended when Eric turned eighteen, and his father had made it clear never to expect anything more from him. Gary had buried his feelings of resentment when the children were younger. But now with Eric intruding into his life with Margie, this resentment began to come between him and his wife. As a couple, they had tried to minimize the "his kid/her kid" dynamic of their family. But unable to let go of the resentment he felt, Gary now found himself thinking of Eric more and more as "her kid."

Margie felt torn between her husband and her son and passively withdrew. She told Gary she couldn't deal with his criticism of Eric and she refused to talk to him about it.

## The Challenge of Stepparenting
## a Boomerang Kid

Few roles require so much emotional maturity, generosity of spirit, and courage as that of stepparent. Do not underestimate the amount of acceptance, understanding, and giving required for stepparenting. It is a difficult, challenging, and confusing role. One of the problems for Stephanie was that in marrying Brian, whose children were over eighteen, she never expected to actively parent his children. This thinking is common where there are adult children, especially when the children have always lived with the other parent. But it is often unrealistic. If you are a stepparent who has held the expectation that your partner's children would never be much of a factor in your life, you will need to rethink this. If you have married someone who cares about his or her children and those children have a crisis, are in need, and turn to your partner, they will be in your life. This is an essential fact of second marriages: *when you marry someone who has children, even if they are adult children, there is always the strong possibility that you may be required to be involved with those children as a stepparent.* Sometimes it helps in accepting this fact to ask yourself, "Would I really love and respect my spouse if he or she were the kind of person who wouldn't come through for an adult child in a crisis?"

Another common but unrealistic expectation is that the stepparent will love the child as his or her own. Even though a stepparent can certainly love and care for a stepchild, there will never be the same bond the stepparent has with his or her own children. Margie needed to understand how hard it was for Gary to have Eric return home. He needed a great deal of support and appreciation from her to help him with his feelings of resentment.

Margie needed to give Gary her empathy, the special kind of understanding that involves a comprehension of what the other person is feeling even when you yourself have never experienced exactly the same situation. What you tune in to are the feelings, not the circumstances. For example, because you have been afraid at some time in your life, you can understand what another person is feeling when he or she expresses fear. You may not be able to understand the specific reasons the person is afraid, but you can still empathize with the feeling of fear. Margie needed to listen to Gary's feelings of resentment about being the sole support of another adult, to his disappointment that their dreams and future plans were being delayed by his stepson's crisis, and to his frustration about the unfairness of it all. She undoubtedly could have empathized with these feelings if she could have set aside her own guilt that one of her children was the stimulus for the feelings. She might then have shared with Gary her own similar feelings, which could bond rather than divide them in their search for a solution.

Parent and stepparent need to work together like any couple in meeting the needs of the adult child. Because this is often so much more difficult an adjustment for a stepparent, it is especially important to spell out the length of time that the adult child will live with you. In adjusting to difficult situations, it helps to know that they are of limited duration.

The stepparent in particular needs a great deal of help and understanding from his or her partner. In Stephanie's situation, Brian was so consumed with guilt about his daughter that he was insensitive to his wife's feelings. One of his mistakes was to tell Stephanie she had no voice in how he handled Patti. While he expected his wife to be there for Patti in a mothering role, he denied her any role in the decision making. This is a common trap. If the parent expects the stepparent to be emotionally involved with the stepchildren, he or she will also have to agree to listen to the stepparent's feelings and to share problem-solving.

When their son Mark returned home, Howard and Jane experienced a different situation. Howard, fifty-two, owned a small dry-cleaning business in the Boston area. He and Jane, fifty, were eagerly planning a long-awaited trip to Israel when Jane's widowed mother, Velma, seventy-five, had a stroke. Unable to afford the round-the-clock nursing care that Velma required, they brought her home to live with them.

Howard and Jane postponed their trip, a great disappointment to them. Jane had worked with Howard in his business, but with her mother requiring so much care she now stayed home. Not long after Velma's stroke, Howard's parents, who lived nearby, also became more dependent on the couple. His father was showing signs of senility, and his mother had given up driving after cataract surgery. In addition, for the past few years the family had been burdened with high college tuition costs for their three children. Now their oldest son, David, twenty-five, had a promising, if low-paying, job on the staff of one of the city newspapers; their daughter, Beth, twenty-three, was an administrative assistant to a state legislator; and Mark, twenty, their youngest, was a college sophomore.

Mark had a difficult adjustment to college, with grades so poor that he began his sophomore year on academic probation. An immature young man, Mark partied almost every night, skipped many classes, and seemed directionless. At the end of the year, he flunked out.

Jane felt that Howard had always been too hard on Mark. A demanding father with rigidly high expectations for his children, he put a high premium on academic success. Mark felt even a genius could not get his father's approval. Jane had always been sympathetic with Mark's struggles to grow up, and she saw him as fragile and vulnerable.

Howard was furious with his son's academic failure. Jane, disappointed and also angry, felt overwhelmed at the prospect of adapting to yet another dependent person in their household, but, upset and concerned about Mark, she felt a need to protect him from his father's rage.

Unable to find full-time work, Mark got a temporary restaurant job, but continued his pattern of staying out late and partying. One evening Jane overheard one of the raging battles between Howard and Mark and broke down in tears. Emotionally exhausted, she wondered when in her life she would have any time without responsibility for either her parents or her children. That night she told Howard, "I thought that someday we would really have time for ourselves — when is it our turn?"

Howard and Jane had already endured a significant loss of territory and privacy when Velma moved in with them, and suffered the disappointment of having to postpone their eagerly anticipated trip. When Mark returned home, the old conflict between him and his father erupted into open hostility as they engaged in the parent-child struggle of the past. With most of the burden of caring for their aging parents on her shoulders, Jane viewed Mark as one more person for her to take care of. Although she perceived her maternal role as protecting Mark from his father's anger, her resentment toward Mark grew.

Since Jane's anger was directed toward her son, she did not voice her disappointment in Howard for continuing his unbending authoritarian approach to Mark. As long as they remained stuck in these isolating feelings, the couple could not put their heads together to figure out what they were going to do about their son. Both were responding to their individual feelings and felt justified in their own positions. Making a shift from "What do *I* need?" toward "What do *we* need?" would have helped them get closer to a solution. If Jane and Howard could have asked themselves, "What does our home need right now?" and "What does our relationship need right now?" they would have begun to develop a whole new approach. When the focus shifts from "me" to "us," from the individual to the couple, people begin to feel more giving: they are no longer giving in to the other person but giving something to their relationship, an entity of which they are a part. With each partner beginning to give, each partner begins to receive and a more balanced feeling is restored, giving the couple a better chance of resolving their difficulties.

Jane and Howard's home needed

1. Both of them to see Mark as an adult who should take responsibility for his own life (get a full-time job, keep hours during the work week that did not disrupt the family, make plans for a time in the near future when he would be on his own).

2. Jane to stop protecting her son as though he were still a small boy. She needed to leave the two men to work out their own adult relationship.

3. Howard to begin to see his son as a separate individual rather than as an extension of himself, and to let go of his unrealistic expectations for him to excel intellectually. By accepting that Mark was not suited for college, he could have encouraged him toward a more realistic goal, such as choosing a technical skill he could be trained in.

4. Mark to shoulder some of the household burdens by helping with the care of his grandparents and with tasks around the house.

In each case history, the psychological impact on the family when the adult child returned home included the following reactions: disappointment, resentment, anger, guilt, sense of loss, sense of failure, loss of privacy, and stress from the increased financial strain. These are natural and normal responses. In each family the losses were real and significant.

Instinctively, parents want to protect a suffering child — but an adult son or daughter who is suffering is still an adult. He or she may be struggling with a temporary setback, but parents need to shift their thinking to what the young person needs at this stage of life.

Each of these families was stuck in the past. Tom and Ann responded to their daughter's depression by taking care of her and not asking anything of her in return. Kristine, who tried to make up for feeling she had failed her son during the divorce, also presented her son with no adult expectations. Guilt was also a factor in Brian's reaction to his daughter's depression, and he expected nothing of her. Gary and Margie agreed to help Eric without asking anything of him in return, and consequently Gary's resentment grew. While Jane babied her son, Howard rigidly demanded that he shape up, not understanding the kind of help he needed in growing up.

The return home is hard on everyone involved. Most of the problems subsequent to the return are related to the mistake of re-creating old parent-child roles. Usually both sides participate in hanging on to old relationships, the parents by babying and protecting and not asking enough of the adult child, the young person by slipping back into a dependent, helpless role.

The task for parents, and it is a difficult task, is to view the young adult not as a dependent child who needs to be taken care of, but as an adult — a struggling adult who needs their help, but nevertheless an adult for whom they need to have appropriate adult expectations. To do any less would be infantilizing — treating him or her like

a small child, and in the process promoting childlike behavior.

Just as the young adult must finally master the developmental task of separation from the parents, so too must
the parents master the task of letting go. They must learn
to tolerate their adult child's discomfort without intruding
and rescuing, and to place appropriate expectations and
limitations on him or her for which support and care will
be given in return. Just as laws are necessary to an orderly
society, spoken expectations are necessary to harmonious
living. From the first moment the young adult asks to come
home, clear adult-to-adult expectations need to be spelled
out, quid pro quo. This not only facilitates the autonomy
and confidence the young adult needs to achieve separation, but also lessens the impact and the intrusion on the
parents' lives — only fair to them as human beings. As
Robert Frost said, "Home is the place where, when you
have to go there, they have to take you in." This is true in
most cases, but *not* unconditionally.

# TWO

## You Can't Go Home Again

### What Happens to Today's Young Adults
### When They Return Home

IN THOMAS WOLFE'S NOVEL *You Can't Go Home Again*, George Webber returned from Europe and went back to his hometown, where he became terribly disillusioned by what he saw. Not only had the town changed, but George had changed too; and he found out that he couldn't re-create the feelings he had had when he lived there. Things would never be the same again. George learned that even though he might be able to go home physically, emotionally he could never go back.

### Boomerang Kids Disillusioned

Just like George Webber in Wolfe's novel, the young adult today who returns home to live after a period of attempted independence becomes disillusioned. When boomerang kids find out things can never really be the same again, they experience disappointment in several important ways. First, they are confronted with a new view of themselves; second, their eyes are opened about home. The sense of disenchantment, as you might expect, is most apparent in those who move back home because of a crisis or a loss of one kind or another — a broken relationship, loss of a job, flunking or dropping out of school, financial trouble, or emotional problems. However, the same responses, although felt less intensely, are experienced by young adults whose return home is not prompted by a crisis.

All boomerang kids feel some disappointment in themselves about having to return to Mom and Dad at all. Their image of themselves has been shaken. Just what it was that led them home determines the extent to which this image is altered. Many of them are returning home because they have stumbled out there on their own; they haven't been able to make it by themselves. When they face this fact, they are no longer filled with the same youthful confidence they had when they first left the nest. They feel much less capable than they thought they were, and much more dependent. They are forced to rethink the whole idea of who they are.

In our fantasies we sometimes idealize and glamorize the home of our childhood and dream about what it would be like to be back there once again, carefree and footloose. Boomerang kids do this, too, of course, and must necessarily face a second disappointment: that the home in their head doesn't exist anymore, if it ever did.

## Conflicts of Dependence vs. Independence

There is usually a kind of war going on inside most young adults, a conflict played out between two parts of themselves. One part of them really wants to be totally independent from parents: free, strong, confident, self-assured, and secure in the knowledge that they can completely take care of themselves, not needing their parents for anything. But the other part of them wants very much to be taken care of; it yearns for the blissful state of turning everything over to some benevolent presence who will think of everything, take care of everything, nurture, support, protect — meet their every need.

The wish to be a child enfolded in the loving warmth of a mother is a normal wish that lies deeply rooted within every human heart. Sometimes the wish blazes, sometimes it flickers, but it is never extinguished. It's a wish that we all carry to the grave. As a person matures, however, the conflict between dependence and independence becomes more and more manageable, the war softens to a skirmish, and the wish to be taken care of becomes the healthy dependence that is as necessary for intimacy and love as is the basic capacity to trust.

## Acute Conflict in Young Adulthood

The conflict of independence vs. dependence often surfaces most strongly just when a person is about to embark on a new task that represents more responsibility, more autonomy, and more adulthood. Observant parents know that small children seem to go backward, regress a bit, and act very needy right before they take a big step forward. For example, a child who is about to start kindergarten and has been getting dressed without any help for quite some time may suddenly want a parent to help every step of the way, with every button and buckle. In adults the same phenomenon can exist. After receiving an important promotion, a middle-aged woman may become anxious, have trouble sleeping, or start losing things, as if the anxious child within says, "I'm just a little kid that needs to be taken care of; I can't possibly be in charge of the whole sales force!"

Procrastination, absentmindedness, disorganization, and chronic tardiness are all manifestations of the child at work within adults, which resists growing up and functioning independently. For the boomerang kid on the verge of adulthood, moving home itself can constitute such a step backward, and regressive behavior such as failure to keep appointments and putting off job hunting or registering for school is common.

## Fear of Abandonment

The pull toward dependency is deeply ingrained. We think that if we can get someone to take care of us, we can avoid experiencing one of the things that human beings fear the most: *abandonment*. For some people the fear of abandonment is so overwhelming that they avoid all close attachments. They feel they couldn't bear it if they were to get attached to someone, allow themselves to love and be loved, and then have that person leave.

An early loss sometimes may have this effect as it did with Harry, twenty-three, whose grandmother died when he was five. His grandmother had lived with the family and been like another mother to him. After her death he was devastated and clung to his parents. Harry had difficulty in school, developing vague and mysterious pains that often interfered with school attendance. Throughout junior high and high school, he made few close friends and spent most of his time with his parents. Although Harry's mother and father were concerned, they avoided any confrontation about his dependency. Instead, they reassured each other that he was just slow in developing. They were sure this would work itself out by the time he went to college. At the state university, Harry lived in the dorm his first few months but found reasons to drop by his parents' home almost daily. Finally, he moved his belongings back home, explaining that his roommate kept weird hours and that studying in the dorm was impossible. Harry continued to be a loner throughout college; and although he found a job soon after commencement, he did not leave home until his father asked him to move. Still closely attached, he called home repeatedly from work and from his apartment. Saying that his parents were all the friends he needed, he made no attempts to socialize. Absences from work became so numerous that he was eventually asked to leave. Unable to support himself, he moved back home again. Another job, and another attempt at independent living, ended a few months later.

Harry was never able to form other attachments separate from his parents. He feared the discomfort he felt when he was alone — abandonment terror that had never been dealt with throughout his childhood. As long as he was in the security of home, Harry could avoid these feelings; outside, they consumed him. He finally agreed to professional help. In therapy, Harry discovered that he had been afraid to leave home for fear that in his absence something would happen to his parents and he would be abandoned. That same fear had kept him from allowing anyone outside the family ever to become important to him.

The spectre of being abandoned is terrifying because as helpless infants and children we literally cannot live without our parents. We need them for survival. Most of us gradually work our way through this abandonment terror in childhood as we incorporate the presence of our parents, building our internal structure so that we can begin to rely on ourselves. Each new step of development evokes the fear of abandonment; each time a new skill is mastered, this accomplishment is accompanied by the actual loss of the parents' involvement. The infant who learns to drink from a cup loses being held while he or she is fed. The toddler who learns to walk loses being carried. The young adult who gains full independence loses the dependent relationship with his or her parents, and that loss precipitates revisiting the earliest fear of abandonment.

The fear of abandonment often lies underneath all kinds of fears that on the surface appear unrelated. For example, people who fear success don't actually fear the promotion itself and the new responsibility; they fear the world will think they are so competent and capable, so grown up and autonomous, that they will be left alone. They fear that when they are successful, no one will remember they still have needs. Some families reinforce this fear. Some parents are able to be close to their children and respond to them only when they perceive them as being in need or having a problem.

Wanda, age twenty-one, experienced this in her family. "I was the youngest of two children and my older brother, Donnie, was my parents' favorite. When my dad was young he had been quite ill in high school and hadn't been able to participate in sports and school activities. My brother turned out to be a great student, a great athlete — the most perfect son you could have, and my dad really lived vicariously through him. My mother, I think, always valued males more than females, perhaps because she never valued herself very much, and she was really caught up in Donnie's life too. I was very much an 'also ran.' When I was in high school it was clear I would never be able to compete with Donnie, but I certainly found other ways to get my parents' attention. I was unhappy and anxious and I gained an enormous amount of weight. I didn't do it consciously, of course, but, nevertheless, it was successful: almost fifty pounds certainly got their attention! My parents were constantly yelling about my eating, putting me on diets, worrying about my weight, and dragging me around to doctors. Our home was in Cincinnati, and after college, where I continued to gain weight, I moved to Cleveland. It was a real turning point for me. I got into therapy, and after two years I lost seventy-five pounds. I got a job I really liked and I started dating. It was scary at first, but I felt like I was finally growing up. At Christmas the first year I lost the weight, Donnie and I were both home for a visit. Donnie hadn't finished college or really done very much with his life. He just wasn't able to make it on his own without my parents; he was always moving back home for a while, then moving out, then moving back. But even though he was no longer the high school hero, my parents were still incredibly involved with him — just the way it had been when we were growing up. Over Christmas, I got more and more anxious each day of the visit and soon I began eating everything in sight — something I hadn't done in a long time. I couldn't figure out what had happened. In spite of everything I worked so hard to achieve — losing the weight, having a job I loved, and for the first time dating and feeling more comfortable with men — I just felt like a mess. It was like I was back to square one, with my parents yelling at me for eating just like I was in high school again. I couldn't believe it.

"When I got back to Cleveland my therapist helped me understand that in being back with my family I had felt something called a regressive pull. It meant that while I observed Donnie having this special relationship with my parents I felt the old feelings I had as a child, and I was pulled backwards into my old behavior to get my parents' attention. We were all back in our places. My success at losing weight and not having a problem anymore scared me, because when I was a capable and successful person I felt abandoned by my parents. So I acted out in the old way to get their attention to ward off the awful empty loneliness I had felt my whole life around Donnie and my dad."

## *Changes in Young Adults' Self-Image*

Young adults who return home often feel a strong wish to
be taken care of and may initially idealize home, but soon
they are confronted with the undeniable fact that they can
never go back to childhood. That safe place, isolated from
the demands of the adult world, is an illusion quickly shattered. The young adult who returns home is contending,
then, with a shattered illusion of childhood and a diminished idea of him- or herself. Sara, twenty, was a typical
boomerang kid in the way she experienced this change in
self-perception.

"When I first moved out, it was just this incredibly exciting time. I had lived at home for two years after high
school while I went to the community college, and when
I graduated I got a job in the trust department of a bank.
It's the same job I have now, a secretarial job, but eventually I'll have an opportunity to start handling some accounts. I really like it.

"When I first started working at the bank, I got to be
good friends with Karen, a woman who worked in personnel. She was about my age and we really hit it off. She
was still living at home, just like I was, but we both wanted
to move out. We talked about it all the time, every day at
lunch and a lot of times when we'd have a beer after work.
Finally it just seemed like a good idea to try and find a
place together. It didn't take us too long to find a great
apartment in Seattle we both liked. I could never have
afforded to live there on my own, but with the two of us
splitting the rent, it was possible and we could make it.
The apartment was unfurnished, and we each scrounged
up some old furniture from our parents. Karen and I had
a great time getting the rest of the stuff we needed at the
Salvation Army and places like that. My parents helped
me move out, and I was a little sad when I left my room

with its beanbag chair and the stuffed animals that I'd had forever all piled in the corner, but the main thing I felt was excitement.

"Karen and I had a fantastic party after we got moved in and all settled. It's hard to describe the feeling I had the first few weeks I lived there. I suppose it was kind of like when I first got my driver's license and took the car out by myself for the first time. Just this incredible feeling of freedom. I was really in charge of my life. I had a job I liked, my own apartment with a great roommate, the apartment was only a few blocks from the lake, there were even some cute guys in our building — it just couldn't have been better. I felt like I had the world by the tail!

"After we'd lived there for a few months, Karen and I started going to Happy Hour at the bar in a restaurant on the lake not too far from our apartment. We met some guys who seemed pretty nice, and they asked us if we wanted to go sailing with them one weekend. We weren't sure if they were serious, but Karen gave them our phone number and it wasn't too long before we heard from them. One of the guys, Bill, was about thirty, and the boat belonged to him. The other guy, Dave, was nice enough, and although I had an okay time I didn't really want to see him again — but Karen really went for this guy Bill. After that first Saturday she dumped everyone else she had been seeing and started this intense thing with Bill. He was always hanging around our apartment, he spent the night every weekend, and I started getting a little irritated having to wait for the bathroom in the morning if Bill was in there — although I suppose I could have adjusted to that if that had been the only problem. But it wasn't. Bill was into cocaine, and pretty soon Karen was, too. At first it didn't seem to interfere all that much. But after a few months she started missing work, and then she started

getting behind in the rent. I would loan her share to her
and she'd promise to pay me back. Of course she didn't,
but I was so naive I believed she would. I ended up using
up all the savings I had, which wasn't that much, just to
cover her half of the rent. Then she got fired from the bank.
It was really awful. My savings were gone and without her
share we couldn't pay the whole amount of the rent. Karen
tried to tell the landlord that she was just temporarily out
of work, but he wasn't having any of that, and next thing
I knew we got an eviction notice.

"My dad helped me pile my half of the furniture into a
trailer he had hitched to the car and off I went, back home.
I had only been on my own seven months! Even though I
tried to tell myself that it was Karen's fault that everything
got screwed up, there I was back in my room with the
beanbag chair and the stuffed animals. I had felt so full of
confidence when I moved out, and now here I was with
my parents again, questioning my judgment, my choice of
friends, my ability to make decisions, to handle myself. I
felt like a little kid. It was as though I had driven the car
for the first time by myself and some jerk had crashed into
me, and I found out real quick that it was dangerous out
there on the streets. I started wondering if I could handle it."

When Sara first moved out she was excited, and savored
her first real taste of adulthood. She loved the freedom she
felt and had every confidence that she could make her way
in the world without having to rely on her parents. When
she and Karen received the eviction notice and she had to
move back home to live with her parents, she felt almost
as though she had been evicted from the adult world. She
had to face the fact that she again needed her parents, and
it was a blow to her self-esteem. The idea of herself as
someone who could manage on her own had been shattered.

*     *     *

Donald was a young adult whose problems growing up were manifested in unsuccessful performance in school. He flunked out of college after his sophomore year and returned home to live with his parents in Berkeley.

"Sometimes I don't know if I really had been ready for college in the first place. Maybe that's wrong, maybe it wasn't college I wasn't ready for — maybe it was life! What I mean is that I had pretty good grades in high school, I wasn't genius material or anything like that, but I had better than a B average. I lettered in cross-country and hung around a lot of guys from the team. It looked like I was pretty well adjusted and that I would make friends, get good grades, and generally hack it in college. Actually, I was well adjusted, I guess you'd say, all except for one area — females. I was terrified of them and had never been involved in a relationship all through high school. In fact, I didn't get involved with anyone until my sophomore year in college. Some of my friends and I solved the virginity problem our freshman year with prostitutes, and although that demystified things a bit, it was kind of sleazy and I still hadn't ever really gone out with a girl. I was starting to wonder if I was some kind of pervert, if I could only make it with a prostitute. I had heard that there were men like that, and I really was beginning to worry that there might be something wrong with me.

"My sophomore year, I lived in a coed dorm and a girl in my eight o'clock anthropology class lived at the end of my floor. Her name was Diane. She was really pretty. We started walking to class together, and I was surprised at how easy she was to talk to — maybe at eight o'clock in the morning I was too sleepy to be nervous. Then we started studying together; pretty soon we were doing everything together, and I knew I was in love with her. I wanted to be with her every minute. I had trouble eating and sleeping, I couldn't concentrate, the whole thing was amazing. Diane said she thought she loved me — well, actually, she said she knew she loved being with me but she said she was kind of confused about the whole thing. She had a boy-friend from last year who wasn't on campus this year, and she was still involved with him. The guy was in England for a semester-abroad program, and they wrote each other all the time. I didn't like it that she was still involved with him, but I tried not to think about it. Sometimes she'd talk about being mixed up, especially after we'd have sex, but I just blocked it out. Diane was my whole life, I didn't care about anything but her, not school, not anything, and I began to get behind on studying. My grades were so bad that at the end of the semester I was put on probation. Second semester everything hit the fan. Her old boyfriend came back to campus, and she started seeing both of us until I got so possessive and jealous that she dumped me. I just went crazy. I mean we lived on the same goddam floor, and I had to put up with seeing this guy come out of her room. I couldn't stand it. One time I thought she was alone in her room, I walked down the hall to see her and knocked on her door. I thought I heard her in there so I opened the door and found her in bed with him. I wanted to kill both of them. I got wasted that night, and if my roommate hadn't been with me I don't know what I would have done. The rest of the semester was a joke. I spent most of it getting drunk. I hardly ever made it to class, and I flunked out.

"It was weird how I felt when I flunked out; in a strange way it was kind of a relief. All I wanted to do was go home and get away from the dorm and Diane. I wanted to hole up in my room at home and just listen to my stereo and look at all the posters I had on the walls of the New York Marathon winners. I wanted to hang out with Mom and Dad and have everything be simple like it used to be before I got mixed up with Diane. I guess I wanted to be a little kid again. I felt lousy about flunking out, but frankly that wasn't the main thing that bothered me. My grades had been okay before I met Diane, and I knew I could do college work. The thing that really tore me up was the feeling that I couldn't compete as a man. It was the first relationship I'd ever had, and I'd been dumped. Whatever confidence I'd had in being able to be involved with a girl went down the tube. As I got ready to leave campus, I started to really build up home in my mind, like it would be easy and simple there. And actually it did feel good to be there for the first few days. Mom and Dad were pretty understanding at first, but it didn't last that long. They started putting pressure on me to get my act together, they were pissed about my blowing a whole semester's tuition money, and I realized that this safe, secure place was something that really didn't exist anymore, I couldn't go back and be like that inexperienced high school kid and pretend that Diane never happened. I wasn't ten, I was twenty, and I did have to get my act together."

Donald's idealized view of home helped him manage his feelings about loss and the rejection by Diane. But he was very quickly disillusioned, confronted by his parents with the undeniable fact of his adulthood. He found that "home" was only a safe and comfortable place preserved in his mind, and "going home" was something he could do only in his fantasies.

Young adults who return home have suffered quite a blow to their self-confidence. They've found their new untested wings not up to the job of full flight, and they come back home feeling inadequate and ashamed. Although some of them may defend against these feelings by assuming a false bravado, most of them have trouble holding their heads up. Their self-esteem, their concept of who they are, is shaken to the core; and they present themselves at the door, wounded and hurting.

The initial response of most parents is to get out the Band-Aids. They feel an overwhelming urge to protect and nurture, to take care of their offspring. This instinctive response arises from the very heart of a parent confronted with a child in pain. The knee-jerk reflex to protect is biological, and neither the age of the parent nor the age of the child diminishes it . But acknowledging this impulse and acting on it are two very different things. Babying these struggling young adults not only works against their best interest, it stunts their growth. It denies them a valuable lesson necessary to continued adult development.

## The Trying Twenties

People in their twenties have developmental tasks to be mastered just as young children do. In her book *Passages,* which popularized theories and studies of adult development, author Gail Sheehy labeled this age the "trying twenties." Why is this such a trying time? Because young adults are sorting through so many options, making decisions about values, life-style, occupation, and choice of a mate, to name just a few. Facing decisions that will affect the rest of their lives, they are also in the middle of one of the most difficult transitions of all: separating from the family and leaving Mom and Dad.

Two specific tasks young people of this age face are the development of a personal identity and the attainment of intimacy. And the two are closely related. Unless a person has a well-defined identity, he or she is sure to be confused about the mysteries of love and intimacy.

## Development of a Personal Identity

In understanding the development of identity that your adult child faces, it's useful to review the process in terms of your own young adulthood and what was required of you at that time in your life.

Identity, which begins at home with one's parents, means knowing who you are as opposed to who they are. Psychologists call the process "individuating," developing a solid sense of who you are as an individual, separate from those around you. The values you decide on and the choices you make are as nearly as possible determined by what you, and you alone, think and feel. Once you are pretty much able to let go of trying to please your parents, or needing to rebel against them by doing just the opposite of what you think they want you to do, you're in a position to go about the business of knowing who you are and standing up for what you believe in. You can now claim a personal identity mostly independent of the programming you've had from your parents. This can be described as moving down a cafeteria line, stopping to pick out what you want, passing by what doesn't appeal to you. You may well choose values, opinions, and standards that are similar to the ones your parents offered. For example, you may decide to accept the religious values and philosophy of life with which you were raised, but if you make this choice as an adult, selecting from all the many options, your choice will reflect your own thoughts and feelings. You make a selection you believe in, and have not just blindly accepted what your parents once decided for you.

On the other hand, there may be a lot about your parents' life-style or beliefs that you decide just isn't for you. You may discover that there are different ways you want to live your life from the way they've lived theirs.

Claiming identity involves understanding that you are separate and different from your parents, even when you may end up choosing to keep for yourself some of the ideas, values, or aspects of the life-style with which you were raised. The most important questions to be answered are

Who am *I*? (not, "Who do my parents want me to be?")
What do *I* want out of life?
What do *I* think?
What is important to *me*?
How do *I* want to spend my time?
What job do *I* want?
What kind of people do *I* like?
What kind of person will *I* love?

## Attaining Intimacy

The last question above — "What kind of person will I love?" — addresses the other important developmental task of young adulthood: intimacy. And the reason it is so closely tied to identity may be best explained if we go back a few years to adolescence and those first relationships.

Teenagers are just beginning to get a sense of themselves as male or female in the first stirrings they feel for the opposite sex. They yearn to be noticed and appreciated, and to have their fledgling sexual identity validated by the opposite sex. If a girl has a crush on a boy and he notices her, pays attention to her, and flirts with her, she feels that her femaleness has been mirrored by his positive attention toward her. It doesn't matter a whole lot who the boy is; the attention of almost any boy will serve this purpose as long as he is someone who has the stamp of approval of her peer group. These attachments, although felt intensely, are early explorations with the opposite sex. Trying on these relationships is much like trying on coats for size. As young people mature, they want to find a relationship that will wear well over time. In order to do that, just like finding a coat that will fit, they have to know what size they are in the first place. They have to have a good sense of their own identity before they can choose an intimate partner to fit them.

Intimacy, the process of learning to love, is a lifelong struggle, and no small task. Just think of all that is required to share one's life with another human being!

First, the whole business begins with a physical and an emotional attraction. Then partners need to have compatible and complementary temperaments. They need to share essentially the same values, respect one another, and have compatible as well as similar goals. They must learn to share territory and work together with a sense of mutuality at the ordinary business of everyday living. They must learn to be open and vulnerable before the other, which requires the ability to trust. They know that the other genuinely wants to meet many of their needs, but that they, and they alone, are responsible for their own happiness. They can have joint and separate interests, and must respect each other's differences and allow for separateness within the relationship. They must learn to honor the other's need for privacy and individual interests and friendships without feeling threatened. They must accept the fact that some conflict is inevitable, and also that they must continually work on developing the skills to resolve conflict without intentionally injuring the other. They must be willing to allow the other person and the relationship to be the center of their lives without having it engulf their existence as separate beings. Successful partners must be able to be kind to each other, to laugh together, and, most of all, to forgive each other. They must learn to be companions, friends, and lovers in the fullest sense, often a task beyond the emotional maturity of large numbers of adults. And the job of learning how to do all of this necessarily begins in earnest in the twenties.

In *Adaptation to Life,* his excellent study of adult development, George E. Vaillant observed that psychiatrists who work with young adults discover that problems with intimacy are the major themes in their patients' struggles.

Regardless of the specific diagnosis, feelings of anguish, pain, or anger because of unsuccessful close relationships are reflected in the serious emotional problems that first strike in young adulthood — schizophrenia, mania, impulsive delinquency, and suicidal thoughts and behavior.[1] For many other young adults not under psychiatric care, disappointing attempts at intimacy often send them boomeranging back home as well.

## Growing Up, a Mourning Process

Growing up, as child psychiatrist Margaret Mahler has said, is really a gradual growing away. It is growing away from the very first loved ones, the parents. Mahler observed that the growing away process is a lifelong mourning process.[2]

This mourning process, the kind of grief that accompanies any major loss, shows itself in adolescence and young adulthood as an underlying normal and predictable depression. As teenagers grow away from their parents, they often become depressed, moody, and irritable. They are reacting to the loss of childhood and the loss of being mothered.

In order to make a successful transition from childhood to full adulthood, human beings need to replace their first loved ones, their parents, with a mate. George Vaillant has written that we stop growing when we don't replace our human losses. Observing that the seeds of love must be eternally resown, he stated that without love it is hard to grow.[3] In the process of replacing the loss of parents, young adults pair with someone with whom they can experience the nurturing and protection they first felt as children. This is where that task of intimacy comes in again and why mastering it is so important to the further growth of human beings. It should be noted, however, that marriage and pairing are not the only routes to growth:

> Obviously marriage is not the be-all and end-all of intimacy; it is merely a tangible marker that flags that invisible, ineffable human process called love. In other cultures and at other points in history, alternative markers of intimacy would have to be used. The church, the teaching professions, and perhaps the armed forces contain highly generative individuals with clear Career Consolidation who have never married. In their twenties, many such men and women have experienced real difficulty with intimacy, yet over the years they have managed to give richly of themselves to the next generation and to grow in the process. I suspect it is not coincidence that such individuals all achieve strong group allegiance, as if the security of group membership provides them the security and strength that most adults find in one-to-one intimacy.[4]

As young adults explore relationships hoping to find security and strength in intimacy, they often run smack into disappointments and rejection. Ideally, they are supposed to be able to handle the inevitable rough times that life dishes out, not by boomeranging home to live with their parents, but by finding comfort from a nurturing presence they have developed inside themselves.

## Developing a Nurturing Internal Presence

Garrison Keillor, in his wonderful story "Storm Home" from *News from Lake Wobegon*, beautifully describes how this process works for him. He starts by saying, "I'll tell you that when I get scared now, one way that I have of quieting myself down is to think back to when I went into the seventh grade." He then states that at Lake Wobegon High, in the event of a blizzard, the children who lived in the country were assigned "storm homes." These were the homes of families in town where they were to go and spend the night if the buses couldn't take them to their own homes in the country. He was assigned to an elderly couple named the Krugers, who became a loving, comforting presence in his mind. In the story he delights listeners with his fantasies of what it was like at the Krugers' little cottage by the lake, and how wonderful he imagined it would be there with them when they took him in from the storm.

He finally tells the audience that in all the years he attended Lake Wobegon High, a blizzard never came during the week that would have caused him to go to his "storm home." But the Krugers, the kindly elderly couple, loomed large in his imagination, and he always believed he could go there and they would take care of him.

He ends the story by saying, "I often dreamed of going to see them when things got hard. Blizzards aren't the only storms, you know, and not necessarily the worst thing that can happen to a child. . . . I always thought that I could go to the Krugers and I didn't, I guess, because all of my troubles were bearable troubles. But I'm certain that they were more bearable for imagining that the Krugers were there, my storm home, and that I could go see them.

"Whenever things got bad I'd think, well, there's always the Krugers."[5]

"Storm homes" live in people's minds in many different forms. Sometimes they are comforting grandmothers, a favorite teacher, the uncle who thought you were special, the next-door neighbor. For the luckiest people, their own parents provide a "storm home" in their mind by becoming incorporated into their very being as a loving, protective self.

Young adults who return home often find it difficult to sustain and nurture themselves. When parents jump in to "make it all better," they deprive their adult children of the experience of learning to comfort themselves. Parents can be more helpful by taking a stance like "the Krugers" — by comforting from afar as the adult child learns how to make his or her troubles bearable troubles.


## Children of Divorce

A stable and secure childhood goes a long way toward creating this safe place within oneself. And one of the most significant ways that the childhood of Garrison Keillor's generation was different from that of today's young adults is that the mid- to late eighties generation of young adults, more than any previous generation, are the children of divorce.

As children they were, in unprecedented numbers, left by someone very important to them. They have seen the most important relationship a child can witness, that of their parents, endure such wounding that it could not be repaired. *They have seen people stop loving each other.*

The later marriages of this generation may very well be a reflection of difficulties with intimacy traced to the divorces of their parents. Their fear of loss may have contributed to an inability to form attachments, resulting in a series of superficial relationships that are of little help in making the transition from adolescence to adulthood. And many of them may be coming back home because they have not been able to work through some of those important early losses. They are less equipped to pair successfully, and therefore less able to move away emotionally and function independently of their parents. There may be much within them that needs to heal. For young adults who were the children of divorce, the return home may be a last attempt to get what they needed as children, before they must give up childhood and move ahead into their adult lives.

## Childcentric Families

In contrast to any previous generation of parents, the middle- and upper-middle-class parents of today's young adults were the first generation to form childcentric families. Many of them created homes in which The Child became the supreme focus. Meeting a whole slew of complex "needs" of The Child (needs previous generations didn't know existed) became the dominant force in the dynamics of the family. It became a career.

Prior to the sixties, the requirements for being good parents were straightforward and uncomplicated. Being a good father meant being a good provider. A good father supplied his family with food, shelter, and clothing. He brought his paycheck home. He wasn't required to spend any time with his children in order to be a good father; he would, in fact, stand out as a father among fathers if, at one time or another, he attended a ball game with his son, or perhaps took his son once or twice on a fishing trip. It was not expected that he spend any time with a daughter in any prescribed activity in order to be an exceptional father to her.

In order to be a good mother, the mother was supposed to prepare three square meals a day, and keep the home and the clothes clean. Beyond those initial requirements, being good parents also involved teaching a child right from wrong, imparting the value of hard work, and providing religious education through church or synagogue attendance; for those families that could afford it, the parents would really be doing a bang-up job if they provided piano lessons.

Today's young adults were raised in the sixties, when much of society was caught up in exploring, experimenting, rethinking, renewing, and rebelling. The old authoritarian way of parenting — "You'll do it because I said so! . . . The answer is NO! . . . I am your father and what I say goes!" — went right out the window. Parents wanted their children to feel good about themselves, to blossom creatively, artistically, and emotionally in a world ripe with possibility. Marlo Thomas and Friends recorded *Free to Be You and Me*, where children heard that it was okay to feel good about who they were, okay to cry, and okay for William to want a doll; on television, *Sesame Street* was born, where Kermit the Frog sang that it wasn't easy being green; and while visiting his neighborhood, children were reassured by their friend Mr. Rogers they were not going down the drain in the bathtub.

Parents flocked to the schools and demanded that their children's education be open, exciting, and enriched. Children were to learn at their own pace as the concepts of "continuous progress" and "individualized instruction" leaped into the classrooms, and "flunking" went up in smoke. Children were never supposed to experience failure. Instead of facing serious consequences for not producing a prescribed amount of work, they found they could usually talk the teacher into giving them another chance by inventing a special project or whipping out an extra report of one kind or another. The special projects and reports often reflected hours of elaborate investment of time, energy, and money on the part of their parents, who, as good parents, were intensely involved in the education of their children.

Parents were involved not only in schools in a way they

never were before, but in after-school activities as well. They felt a pressure to introduce their children to every kind of activity imaginable, and so they chauffeured them in droves to gymnastic lessons, riding lessons, dancing lessons, all kinds of music lessons, painting, pottery, and sculpture lessons. They signed them up for sports: soccer, baseball, football, karate, track, and swimming. As good parents they were supposed to participate themselves, to take a turn at coaching, to help with the uniforms, to bring the oranges for halftime, and especially to attend every single game in order to beam at and cheer for The Child.

In the middle of all this activity, something happened within the head of The Child. The Child got the idea that he or she was indeed *The Center Of The Universe*. Unfortunately, this feeling does not help one adapt to a real world filled with setbacks, disappointments, consequences, and losses, a world where people get evicted from apartments, fired from jobs, and dumped in relationships. The mindset of the depression-era generation, when life was *expected* to be a struggle, actually equipped its young adults much better for life in the real world.

Feeling that one is the center of the universe also does not prepare a person to meet the demands of an intimate relationship, which requires compromise, negotiation, an extraordinary capacity to give, and caring as deeply for another as one does for oneself.

While today's young adults were children of plenty, they have been deprived of something crucial to the full, rich life their parents sacrificed so much to ensure for them. Their well-intentioned parents thought they were providing the nutrients for their children's growth and blossoming, enabling them to do what America did in 1969: reach for the moon. In fact, when they deprived them of struggle, of the private joy of mastery that was independent of recognition from others, of suffering consequences and learning from them, of the pain of failure, they stunted their growth. Always having someone there to bail them out, these young people were denied the growth-producing experiences of problem solving on their own; and as a result many of them lack the tools and the confidence to make it without their parents' continued support. Instead of feeling good about themselves, instead of holding themselves in high esteem as their parents had hoped, they feel fragile, insecure, and resentfully dependent on Mom and Dad. Instead of moving full-speed ahead on their way to having it all, when they meet their first disappointments they often come boomeranging home.

## Narcissistic Entitlement

Some of these young adults have the feeling that they are special, and entitled to have everything they want come their way without effort on their part. In her excellent overview of today's young adults, *The Postponed Generation*, Susan Littwin observes that as parents, her generation thought that life would be rich and rewarding for their children. The children were encouraged to express themselves and to seek fulfillment, and parents were sure that somehow sheer abundance would support their sons and daughters. Referring to *Privileged Ones*, the fifth volume in child psychiatrist Robert Coles's Children of Crisis series, Littwin expands the complicated, class-connected psychology of "narcissistic entitlement," which Coles found in the children of the very rich, to include today's middle-class young Americans. She observes that these young people, like the children born to wealth and power in Coles's study, put tremendous emphasis on the self; have a distaste for answering to others; believe that, magically, things will work out the way they want them to, that their fantasies will come true, and that the world they move in will be strung with safety nets. Littwin concludes that these are not unreasonable ideas for children who will inherit wealth and social position, but that they are dangerous illusions for everyone else.[6]

## What Adult Children Need from Parents

When adult children return home, both they and their parents have a great deal of unfinished business to complete. Coming home with their shattered illusions about the world and their place in it, adult children must learn to handle disappointment and failure, something they were protected from while growing up.

To the question "What do our adult children need from us during this time?" we answer that "they need you to start with them where they are: confused, injured, disillusioned, embarrassed, floundering, ashamed." They need

1. Your empathy. Try to change places with them in your thinking; walk around in their shoes for a bit, remembering what it feels like to have something go terribly wrong. How did you feel when a relationship didn't work out, when you lost a job or failed at something that was important to you? Recall those feelings so that you can emotionally tune in to what your adult child is feeling. Try to appreciate the differences between your child's upbringing and yours, what a confusing and complicated job separating is when you haven't had the natural rites of passage to give you practice and support. Remember that while your adult child may have had many more privileges and benefits than you did, he or she also missed out on some of the struggles vital to maturity.

2. A new viewpoint. Let them know that you consider this return a temporary setback, not a permanent failure, and that their stay with you is preparation for once again living on their own. Emphasize that they will be living in your home under different conditions from those of their childhood.

3. Encouragement to develop confidence and competence. Both of these are acquired in the same way: by one's own efforts. Confidence comes as a result of succeeding at life's tasks, and competence comes with practice. Young people need to overcome obstacles on their own to feel confident and competent. Parents who give warm, genuine support to young adults' efforts toward autonomy encourage them to take initiative; and when they require them to contribute something of value to the household, they add to their self-esteem. Young people then feel they have something to offer in return for the second chance they are being given. They feel important, and needed, and more like the adults they really are.

4. Respect for autonomy. By having realistic, adult-level expectations that you and your adult child have worked out together, you enhance the sense of confidence and competence you are encouraging. Avoid doing anything for young adults that they can do for themselves. Ideally, the effective mother teaches by first demonstrating how to do the task to be mastered, then by letting the child try it alone, moving from coach to cheerleader. She teaches her small son to tie his shoe by showing him how, perhaps several times, before she guides his hands through the exercise again and again. Finally, she watches on the sidelines and allows him to struggle with the task alone. She cheers him on, but she doesn't tie the shoe for him; she lets him work through his frustration without interference. Finally,

she applauds his victory as he beams with confidence at his new competence.

Parents are, in fact, preventing growth if they are doing boomerang kids' laundry, cooking their meals, cleaning their rooms, paying their bills, and expecting nothing in return. When parents stop treating these young adults as helpless children, boomerang kids will eventually start behaving like competent adults.

5. Acceptance of their emotional responses. Knowing that some depression is a normal and predictable part of the regression that the young adults experience is reassuring to both of you; allowing them some time to be sad, to feel their feelings, not only is vital to their understanding of what happened in their lives but will speed their return to independence. Most young adults naturally do some bouncing around, moving forward, falling back a bit, getting discouraged, feeling confused occasionally, as they struggle to get their lives together. One of your most difficult tasks is to stand by and allow the young adult to be uncomfortable. The trick is to find the delicate balance that is supportive without being overprotective, tipped well in the direction of a hands-off position. Giving comfort is important, something you would do for a friend, but if you see your role as *needing* to be there every minute, you will once again deprive your adult child of learning to meet his or her own emotional needs. When you offer empathy and understanding, you allow them to develop inside themselves a warm, comforting presence, a nurturing self-parent they can carry with them wherever they go, forever.

One of the most valuable gifts we offer our adult children is the encouragement of autonomy. None of us parents

perfectly — "perfect" doesn't exist — but we can try to
remember that encouraging autonomy means

> *To empathize without infantilizing*
> *To support without controlling*
> *To give them what they need*
> *So they no longer need you.*

# THREE

# No Free Lunch

*Teaching the Young Adult*
*About Life in the Real World*

NO FREE LUNCH . . . or dinner, or breakfast, for that matter. In this world there really is a price for almost everything, and the purpose of allowing young adults to return home is to prepare them to make their way in the world — without you. The best way to do this is to duplicate as much as possible a real-world situation for them in your home. An exchange is called for: room and board in exchange for money. That's how the world works. If the boomerang kid temporarily has no money, then the barter system is in order: room and board in exchange for specific services in lieu of rent money.

Each young adult returning home should be expected to earn money in some way to gradually contribute to his or her own support while living with parents. Not only does this work toward the goal of leaving home again as an independent person, but, just as important, it also helps the young person see him- or herself as a capable, contributing human being. Work and love are the two crucial ingredients to a satisfying life; the workplace is where we feel worthwhile, get recognition from others, feel productive, and earn money with which to support ourselves.

Young adults who have not been able to support themselves while living independently can use this time at home to manage their finances in a more realistic way, perhaps for the first time learning to live on a budget, balance a checkbook, and put aside a percentage of each month's income as savings.

## It's Your House

There is one fundamental fact that must serve as the foundation for all talks with the young adult who wants to return home and that must be understood by everyone. It is the nonnegotiable, undisputed fact that *IT'S YOUR HOUSE* and *you* get to make the house rules.

The idea of rules of the house need not negate the idea of adult-to-adult communication with boomerang kids. We're not suggesting making all kinds of rules, as if these young adults were little kids. But the world functions with order and expectations. An employer expects you to get to work on time. The landlady expects you to pay the rent. Everywhere in the adult world there are rules. Home is no exception.

Even though the adult child is paying rent or providing some services instead of rent money, this does not set up a situation of equal rights. The balance of power lies with the parents, just as it always does with a landlady or landlord or an employer. Young adults may not like this situation very much; they may long for the time when they have their own place again and can leave dishes piled up for days, have friends over whenever they feel like it, make love in the middle of the living room if they want, talk on the phone as long as they choose, play their music as loud as they like, and in general not have to answer to anyone. That, of course, is as it should be when they're off on their own. But now they are in your house. They don't have to *like* living by the rules of the house, but they do have to go along with your wishes for sharing the territory if they expect to live with you.

You don't have to feel guilty about setting up guidelines for the way the house will operate. It's your house. If you say "no smoking," that's what it will be. There are plenty of shared housing situations with policies like "no smoking." This also applies to having overnight guests. If you don't allow them, then that's it. We feel that your adult child's sexuality and relationships are none of your business (we'll discuss this in detail in the next chapter), but having an additional body in your house is an issue that you do have something to say about.

A little grumbling on their part about your house policies is par for the course, remember, and, after all, you don't want your adult children finding it *so* comfortable at home that they stay with you forever. A scene in *The Breakfast Club*, a movie that was both funny and sad, has a group of high schoolers spending Saturday morning in detention hall as a penalty for rules infractions. One young man complains across the table to a friend that he doesn't get along with his parents, and the friend says, "Of course you don't get along with them; if you did, you'd never want to leave home!"

Parents who allow their adult children carte blanche to do whatever and whenever they please may unconsciously not want them to leave. Often they are avoiding facing their own loneliness or a marriage that may leave a lot to be desired.

## Spelling Out Conditions

When your adult child asks if he or she can move back home, and if it is okay with you, we advise that you answer,

"Yes — on certain conditions." From the very first moment, it needs to be clearly spelled out that boomerang kids will have to agree to certain conditions if they want to live in their parents' house. They need to understand what those conditions are; if they feel they can accept those conditions, then they can move in.

*Before* you meet with your adult child, you need to figure out just what conditions will make you comfortable. Ask yourselves how much rent you feel is reasonable, or, if your adult child has no income, what services you might accept in lieu of rent. Decide what you expect in terms of meals. Should they be shared? Will you take turns cooking? Will you each cook for yourselves and only occasionally share a meal? Who will grocery shop? Who will wash the dishes? How will you handle other household chores? What conditions do you have for use of the telephone, the stereo, the television? Will you allow guests, and if so, under what conditions? What about transportation? Are you willing to share your car? If so, under what conditions? If not, what then?

If you are a single parent living alone, you will decide these issues for yourself. If you have a partner or a spouse, adding another person to your household will go more smoothly if the two of you can reach a common understanding on these issues before the adult child comes home. Often one partner has more definite expectations than the other. Often, too, you will have different levels of tolerance for the personal habits of your adult child. You may not be able to stand wet towels left on the bathroom floor, while your husband simply kicks them out of the way, unconcerned. Or he can't stand a houseful of your son's friends visiting when he comes home from work, while you don't particularly mind the noise. All these little things are exactly the issues that can mushroom into conflict and produce a level of tension that is anything but little. The couples who are the most successful, both in their relationship with one another and in dealing with their boomerang kid, are those who are sensitive to each other's differences and concerned about each other's comfort. The father who, left alone, couldn't care less about the wet towels makes it a family concern because he knows it bothers his wife.

If you have other children at home, or if you have elderly parents living with you, it's important to consider the needs of the entire family. Given the way the household has been operating, how can your returning son or daughter help with some of the duties the rest of you have been sharing?

Once you've worked out your own expectations of how this additional person will fit in with the household, you need to meet with your adult child and state your conditions clearly. Stating your conditions and talking them out sounds simple — but it isn't. Especially if you haven't had a lot of practice. You will make it much easier for yourself if you have thought them out clearly and agreed on them with your partner *before* you sit down to discuss them with your son or daughter. When parents haven't thought about the impact a returning son or daughter will have on their life-style beforehand, they usually have a hard time expressing their feelings after the problems arise. Most of us have had the experience of trying to assemble something without first reading the directions, only to find the task impossible and ending up feeling frustrated and angry. Finally, we grab the written instructions in desperation. If only we had done that first! You can avoid a parallel situation by working out beforehand a set of guidelines that will ease the effect on everyone when your adult child returns home.

## *The Rent*

The first thing you need to establish is the rent. Your adult child needs to know not only what sum you feel is reasonable, but exactly when you want to receive it. Try to duplicate conditions in the real world wherever possible. If your adult child has no income, discuss services that might be offered in lieu of rent. Among the possibilities are cooking, cleaning, household repairs, painting, gardening, car maintenance, running errands, doing laundry, scheduling appointments by phone, gathering information, shopping, sewing, or any other skills within the capability of the young adult. Some of the boomerang families who had the least amount of conflict were those who put the specifics of their arrangement in writing, drawing up a list of the services the young adult would perform.

## *Sharing Household Tasks*

The young adult needs to share in running the house as a fully participating adult. There are many approaches to dividing the household tasks equitably. One that has worked well for many boomerang families involves drawing up a list of all the jobs required to run the house. Each family member takes a copy of the list and makes three columns ("I want to," "I don't want to," and "I don't mind"), putting each task under the appropriate column.

| I want to | I don't want to | I don't mind |
|-----------|-----------------|--------------|
| Wash car | Mow grass | Washing dishes |
| Wash dog | Clean toilets | Raking leaves |

The family can then together work out a system whereby members have a balance of the tasks they want, those they hate, and those they don't mind. This self-selection process results in many of the tasks that some family members dislike being easily chosen by others. Those that nobody likes can be alternated or traded on a weekly basis so that nobody gets stuck permanently with a hated job.

An alternate approach is to write each household task on a separate piece of paper; each family member draws from the hat. You can negotiate with each other and trade tasks; you may even have a laugh or two in the process. ("I'll trade you one week of toilets for two weeks of grocery shopping.") You can also decide to live with the "hand you were dealt," but hold a new drawing every few weeks to give everyone a new set of tasks.

## *When Other, Younger Siblings Are Living at Home*

The need for clearly defined conditions is especially acute when there are younger siblings living at home. The seventeen-year-old brother of a boomerang kid described the situation when his older brother moved back home: "When my brother, Bob, left for college I got to move into his room. It's in the basement and has a separate entrance. I really liked having that room. I also got to drive the old clunker that Dad had around for us kids. I'm the youngest, and it was great having it all to myself. Bob dropped out of college, and when he came back home he wanted his old room back. He also thought he could drive the car whenever he damn well pleased — I was really mad. If my parents hadn't made us sit down and figure the whole thing out, I think we would have gotten seriously physical — we're talking violence here!"

A younger sibling, particularly a teenager, experiences

a significant loss of territory when an older sister or brother boomerangs home. If your family is in this situation, we recommend the following:

1. Make sure the territory of the younger sibling is honored. He or she should not be displaced because an older sibling has returned. It is up to the older sibling to adapt to the family as it now operates, which means that the older sibling does not get his or her old room back if it has been taken over by someone else.
2. Negotiate schedules for use of the car, and work out compromises where necessary. However, the scale should be balanced in favor of the younger sibling. (For example, during the week of the senior prom the younger sibling may need the car more often.)
3. Inform younger siblings of the conditions that have been set for the older sister or brother. Knowing that the older one has to pay rent or contribute services in lieu of rent makes the loss of territory easier to swallow for the siblings still living at home.

If your adult child has returned home because of emotional difficulties, younger siblings may need help in understanding the nature of the disturbance and in coping with it. If you don't feel able to supply this help yourself, don't hesitate to seek family therapy. A discussion of the common emotional problems affecting young adults and the indications for seeking professional help are covered in chapter six.

## When the Adult Child Returns Because of Illness

If your adult son or daughter returns home because of an illness that prevents him or her from independent functioning, you will feel an ever greater pull toward old parent-child roles. In this situation your adult child _is_ authentically dependent on you to meet all kinds of needs.

As your adult child beings to get well, it's important to increase your expectations based on his or her improving capacity for activity. He or she needs to feel competent again and capable of pulling his or her weight as much as possible. Consider all the many nonstrenuous household tasks and long-delayed projects you have, and ask your adult child to help you with them. Paying bills, filing, polishing silver, sewing on buttons, mending, and making photo albums are just a few of the things convalescents can do. As your adult child gets stronger, you can expect him or her to meet more individual daily needs, such as fixing meals and doing laundry.

It is not easy to have expectations of adult children who have been ill; they have often regressed during the illness, and even though they are getting better, they may want to continue to be taken care of, making it difficult for you to pull back from such a familiar parental care-giving role. But adult expectations are just as necessary in this situation as they are for healthy adult children who return home. If more and more is required of them, convalescing adult children can avoid an extended regression into dependency during this crucial stage in their development.

## Contracts

Mary, age forty-seven, a Houston lawyer, was a single parent who thought consideration for one another was a given when her twenty-four-year-old son, Jim, returned to live with her. But all the verbal agreements they made fizzled away, and she was left with all the work. After telling him one too many times that "I thought you knew you were supposed to clean the bathroom," and "I thought you knew you were supposed to pay for your long distance calls," and "I thought you knew I needed quiet time in the evening and not to come home to a houseful of your friends," Mary decided it was time to put her professional knowledge to work. She drew up a contract with Jim to reflect their agreement of the conditions under which he would be living in her home:

### CONTRACT

It is hereby agreed that:

1. Jim will live in his old room, beginning February 1. He will have saved enough money to move out by November 1. He can move out earlier if he would like.

2. He will pay $100 a month for his room and $100 a month for food beginning with his second monthly paycheck.

3. He will be responsible for purchasing and caring for his own clothing, doing his own laundry and sheets and towels, and purchasing items for his personal use.

4. He will pay for his long distance calls.

5. He may have friends over on weekends, but not on weeknights unless with prior consent.

6. He may play his stereo and TV in his room. He agrees to turn the volume down when requested.

7. He agrees to wash the car every Saturday.

8. He will eat breakfast and dinner at home. If he is not coming home for dinner, he will leave a message on the answering machine by 4:00 P.M.

9. He will alternate cooking and grocery shopping with Mom.

| | |
|---|---|
| _____ | _____ |
| Mom | Jim |

| |
|---|
| _____ |
| date |

This turned out to be a good solution for Mary and her son, one that can be useful for other families that have the repeated "misunderstandings" that Mary and Jim had. For those who like this concept, it is probably a good idea to review the contract periodically at a family meeting. No matter how specifically the contract is worked out ahead of time, some unanticipated conflicts and situations will arise. The contract should be a working blueprint for the way the group will function together — not an unchanging document written in stone.

## Finding Personal Comfort

It would be difficult to cover all the different specific areas of a young adult's life that could be of concern to a parent; there are as many as there are people, and they are just as varied. We suggest, however, that you identify potential problem areas and devise a plan for handling them. Comfort is a funny thing: some people love a warm house, and others can't stand anything over sixty-eight degrees; some people need a quiet environment in which to work, and others can be productive listening to rock music; some people can blind themselves to a messy house, and others need neat, orderly surroundings. Find your own comfortable place. When the boomerang kid is doing something that absolutely drives you bonkers, Joan Rivers's line "Can we talk?" comes in handy. Don't ignore your discomfort; talk it out, work it through, compromise where you have to. You have a right to have your home free of the things that irritate you. Your adult child will let you know if he or she thinks you are asking too much or intruding on his or her private space.

The families that have the most trouble adjusting to a boomerang kid are those who have never talked about the situation or come to any agreements as to how all the details would work. The young adult assumes it's his or her home just as it used to be, the parents make the same assumption, and the young person slides back into the family to stay "for a while." Often the weeks turn into months, people begin getting on each other's nerves, and the arrangement begins to sour.

That's exactly what happened when Robert, twenty-four, moved back home after living away for six years. For four of those years he had been in college; for the last two he worked as a salesperson in the lumber industry. When he lost his job and was unable to afford to live on his own, Jack and Ellie, his fifty-six-year-old parents, gave little thought to their immediate answer, "Sure, Robert. Come on home." They had plenty of room in the large, comfortable house that for more than twenty years had been their family residence.

When Robert was in college, Ellie had become interested in raising plants, and now the bright, glassed-in sun room was filled with more than one hundred varieties of greenery. She had furnished the room with white wicker furniture, paving the brick floor herself and making the vivid yellow drapes that framed its windows. She loved the room and every plant in it. It reflected her newfound identity as a separate person, not just a wife and mother, as no room in the house ever had when the children were growing up. Jack found the chairs there uncomfortable. He preferred the family room with its soft leather chairs, and spent evenings there, reading and listening to music in front of the fireplace, or building model boats in a corner filled with all his hobby supplies. Jack often told Ellie, "I'll be in my room," and she knew exactly what he meant.

Robert had struggled not only with his finances while living on his own after college, but with feelings of loneliness. When he lost his job, his only feeling about moving back home was relief. His parents were proud of the fact that he had done well both in college and at his sales job. It certainly wasn't his fault that the lumber industry was so slow. They didn't anticipate any problems with what was to be only a temporary situation, and so neither side talked at all about what the move back home would be like. Robert moved in with a few pieces of furniture and dozens of boxes, piling them in the middle of the family room.

The first indication of trouble was that the boxes stayed exactly where they had originally been dumped. Jack had pushed his chair closer to the fireplace to make room; ignoring the pile, he just walked around it. Ellie suggested to Robert that he might want to use a storage area in the garage for the boxes, but she didn't insist, and the boxes stayed there for another week. Just looking at them every day bothered Ellie.

One day when she came home from volunteering at the hospital and began to tend her plants, she noticed some of Robert's furniture now crowded into the sun room. In the family room Robert had also moved a lot of his father's equipment to make room for his stereo. That night Ellie told her husband that it really upset her to have her room and the family room so crowded and junked up with Robert's stuff — but she felt sorry for Robert because he had lost his job and she felt guilty about being angry. Jack, who had never been very good at handling conflict, busied himself sanding a piece from a model boat. "It will be okay," he told her. "He won't be here long."

Despite following through on some contacts made by his father, Robert was unsuccessful at finding another job. A few weeks became three months. As he continued job hunting, he seemed in fairly good spirits and unaware of his parents' increasing dissatisfaction with his presence. Little things such as Robert's leaving dishes in the sink, late night phone calls, and clothes left in the family room began to loom bigger and bigger. The last straw came when Robert told Ellie he had invited a few friends over. The "few friends" turned into thirty young people partying in the family room and the sun room. Ellie and Jack had reached their limit. Robert was asleep most of the next day. When he finally got out of bed, Ellie tearfully said, "I can't stand this. We have to do something."

*What went wrong?* Robert and his parents represent a fairly typical boomerang triangle. His return interrupted the comfortable routine they had established in their empty nest, a life-style they had come to enjoy. The family did not give careful consideration as to why Robert was coming back home to live, what was to be accomplished, how long it would take, and what the impact on them would be. While Ellie and Jack had sustained a great deal of affection for each other throughout the twenty-nine years of their marriage, they had a way of avoiding the small problems that inevitably cropped up, preferring to let things take their natural course and work themselves out. In the years Robert was growing up and living at home, Ellie had not asked very much of him. She believed it was her job as his mother to take care of him. During the years that he had been away, she had developed a new sense of herself; when Robert came home and slipped into his old role, Ellie was reluctant to slip back into hers. On the surface she behaved as she always had, by not asking much of him; but emotionally this no longer worked for her and she became angry with him. Very good at "looking the other way," Jack and Ellie didn't face conflicts well and were unprepared for the intrusion Robert's return represented.

*What could they have done differently?* When Ellie first noticed her irritation about the boxes left in the middle of the floor, she could have asked Robert directly to store them in the garage. By "suggesting" that he move them, she gave Robert the impression that he could do it when he got around to it. By not confronting his lack of response, she reinforced Robert's feeling that there was no urgency to her request. With her tendency to "overlook" problems that required confrontation, she lived with unnecessary irritation and resentment. Instead of turning to her husband to solve the problem, she could have confronted Robert directly about the furniture he had placed in the sun room and family room.

Marriages thrive and survive through learning and growing. Jack and Ellie could have begun to establish a new way of facing problems, agreeing not to turn away from, ignore, or bury conflict but to work together on mutually satisfactory solutions. They could have reversed the situation with Robert much earlier if they had openly expressed their feelings to each other, sought alternatives, and made reasonable ground rules. Not only would their present life have been improved by this new pattern, but conflicts in future years could have been eased as well.

*What if this approach doesn't work?* Even after ground rules are clearly spelled out, everything does not always run smoothly. If Robert's behavior did not change, Jack and Ellie would have to keep trying, as many times as it took, to achieve results. A simple statement such as "I'm disappointed that I have to tell you again not to leave your clothes in the family room after we agreed you'd keep them picked up" may need to be repeated until the agreement is kept. We all have a tendency to slip back into old habits. Change does not come easily; it takes time and effort. You may become frustrated and feel you are nagging, but the alternative is to allow your adult child to behave immaturely. Most people operate with goodwill toward each other and want to please those they care about, so you will usually get results if you stay with this approach. In most cases, your adult child has simply forgotten that there's a new system in effect and has automatically reverted to old behavior. If your repeated attempts to remind your son or daughter of the agreements you have made are met with hostility and a belligerent unwillingness to change, you may be dealing with someone who is very angry and troubled, and in need of counseling.

The majority of adult children who return home try to be likable, and they mean well; but no matter how easy the relationship might have been while your son or daughter lived independently, you can still expect wrinkles, rips, and even holes in the fabric of your lives with the return home. If you don't spell out your expectations clearly at the beginning, you may find it much harder to make changes later, when they may be complicated by strong, often unpleasant feelings. The weeks and months of very tense living that Jack and Ellie experienced were too long a time to be uncomfortable in their own home.

## Never Too Late to Set Limits

Some parents have trouble with even the idea of setting house policies. Their inability to set limits and lay down ground rules, to even think about saying "no," can come from a variety of sources. Some parents were never very good disciplinarians when their children were small, believing this would inhibit the child's free expression or curb his or her spirit; they couldn't tolerate the idea of making their child unhappy. While we can remember the cute, freewheeling little kid who thought the world and everything in it was there for his or her pleasure, nobody thinks an adult who acts that way is very pleasant to be around. Sometimes it is this attitude on the part of adult children that has made it difficult for them to function effectively in the world away from the family. Setting house policies helps the young adult prepare for reentry into the real world.

Some parents may have such guilt about the role they played in the setbacks their son or daughter may be experiencing that they are unable to place anything close to a demand on him or her now. We have heard parents apologize for having to make rules, "because she is already having such a hard time without us coming down on her." We want to stress that many of the reasons young adults struggle with independence have to do with their inability to live within limits or set their own guidelines. This return home is a unique opportunity for parents to create a model, maybe for the first time, for living within boundaries. It's never too late.

## Talking About Feelings

Many people, men and women alike, have great difficulty expressing their feelings and thoughts, particularly when there is a critical overtone to them. Not all of us came from families where personal feelings and opinions were allowed expression, particularly when ideas and thoughts ran counter to those of the parents. Our parents themselves may never have been allowed to speak out in their own families, and we're simply repeating their history. People who are uncomfortable with conflict often avoid expressing any feelings at all, thus limiting the chance for closeness.

It was like that when Arnie, fifty-six, and his daughter Lise, twenty-nine, lived together. Arnie lived in the same two-bedroom apartment in which he and his wife had raised their two daughters. Since his wife's death three years before, Arnie had been alone with only the family dog for company. When his older daughter, Lise, was widowed, Arnie offered her a room in his apartment, the room she had shared with her sister while growing up. She returned home with eleven boxes of personal belongings and her cat. Arnie and Lise never considered that problems might arise. They never talked about how they would share the limited space, which had now grown even smaller with her arrival. Arnie's solution to the inevitable clashes that followed was simply to change the way he did things, to adapt without complaint. He was a passive man, and even when his wife was alive, there was never any show of emotion between family members. When Lise played her stereo loudly, Arnie just turned up the volume on the television. When the cat and the dog began their usual evening fight, Arnie put the old dog in his bedroom, ignoring the dog's whining and scratching to get out. He felt that Lise shouldn't have to lock the cat up, "she'd already had enough losses." When Lise began dating again and spending evenings at home with her young man, Arnie increasingly went to the neighborhood tavern until bedtime. Although Lise watched her father's gradual retreat and felt uncomfortable, she didn't know how to go about expressing her concern. The tension grew, with Arnie becoming more and more withdrawn. Lise had been in need of comfort and closeness, but Arnie's avoidance of conflict cut off any opportunity for her to get what she needed from him.

Arnie and Lise's dilemma is not unusual. When people avoid conflict, they also avoid the opportunity to work through and solve a problem together. They miss out on the chance to cooperate together and the pleasure that comes from mutual problem solving and teamwork. They lose out on the joy that comes from giving to each other.

Of course, what Arnie and Lise needed was to be able to talk to each other. People aren't mind readers. They need to tell each other how they feel. But this can seem like traveling to a foreign land if you've never done it before. Communication does not come easily and naturally to everyone. When trying to talk about problems face-to-face is too uncomfortable, writing out individual thoughts and feelings, although it may seem a bit awkward, is sometimes one way to get started. Begin with several headings, which may include such subjects as "I feel . . . ," "I think that . . . ," "I want . . . ," "I am concerned about . . . ," "I get upset when . . . ," "It feels unfair when . . . ," "I like . . . ," and "I don't like. . . ." Filling in responses may provide a framework for sharing ideas.

If your family decides to use this list, making it a point of departure in learning how to talk to each other, set a specific time to come together to share the contents of the lists. At first it probably works best to read them to each other without reacting. No feeling or wish or thought or opinion is too trivial or silly or stupid or selfish or unimportant to bring up. Each person is entitled to his or her own feelings and ideas; it is especially important to remember this when family members are sharing this part of themselves for the first time. We are never more vulnerable than when we say, "I want . . . " or "I feel . . ."

Having their feelings listened to without criticism makes people feel cared about and understood, and fosters goodwill and cooperation. Goodwill toward one another, and the experience of simply being in this situation together, expressing and listening to individual needs and wants, is an essential part of the working-through process that will ease the difficult task ahead. Each party's task is to make adjustments to the feelings and needs of the others, through the difficult process of compromise and negotiation. We are not talking about compromise in the area of house policy, things such as rent, smoking, overnight guests, or use of the car. These rules have already been set down by the parents. We are talking about all the unanticipated little things that crop up and cause tension, all the ways people get on each other's nerves — things such as leaving clothes in the washer or dryer; leaving empty toilet paper rolls, hair in the drain, caps off toothpaste, dirty ashtrays; monopolizing the phone, leaving lights on, not filling the gas tank, leaving newspapers on the floor . . . to name just a few. Of course, in areas of dispute, you have the final say because it's your house. While this unequal balance of power is one of the givens of the relationship, remember that the goal here is cooperative living, not a military dictatorship; and for a true sense of harmony both sides in this cooperative venture need to feel satisfied. Therefore, it is important to work toward solutions that are mutually satisfying. Once you have addressed the problem areas as a family and found solutions, everyone will feel a sense of balance.

## Listening to Each Other

Listening is one of the greatest gifts we can give one another. In talking over all your concerns, *listen* to each other. If your son says, "Mom, it really bothers me when you ask me where I'm going every time I go out," try to avoid defensively coming back with "Are you saying I'm nosy? I'm just interested in you." Instead, if you really listen, you will learn what it is about your behavior that bothers your son. You need to answer him by saying something like "I'm sorry. I didn't realize I was stepping on your toes — I'll try not to ask so many questions." You might tell your daughter, "It upsets me never to be able to find the newspaper when I get home from work. After you've read it, I'd appreciate your leaving it on the table in the living room." If she avoids being defensive, she can hear your feelings and see your request as reasonable. She could answer, "I'm sorry it's a hassle. I'll try to remember to put it on the table for you." As parents, you can show adult children you hear what they're telling you by changing your behavior. When they see that you're being thoughtful and considerate, it sets the tone and makes it much easier for them to return thoughtfulness to you.

It's important that both sides realize that continuous talking is an important factor in making communication work. Final results are seldom achieved on the first go-around. It's best not to attempt to cover too much ground at each gathering. Because the subject matter may be difficult, each of you may have complex, unsettling responses; this can be emotionally exhausting. Take breaks, short enough to simply shift gears or long enough to take a walk, eat a meal, or relax in a quiet place alone, leaving with an agreement to return at a specific time to continue.

Talking things over, listening to really *hear* each other, and acknowledging the validity of everyone's feelings are important steps in moving from old parent-child roles to adult-to-adult ties. You have adult expectations of your children for paying rent and pulling their share of the household load. But remember that treating them as adults means not only having adult expectations of them, but in return being sensitive to their feelings and making efforts to adapt to them as you would to any other adult. You are responding as one adult to another when your adult child asks you reasonably to change a bothersome behavior of yours and you try to change it. When your son or daughter asks you to make a reasonable change and you respond by saying, "No . . . I'm your father and I have a right to . . . " you remain stuck in the old role.

## Get to Know Each Other as People

Sharing feelings isn't just for working through conflicts; it's also for getting to know each other as real people. It's often difficult for children to see their parents as real human beings with a full set of concerns, feelings, and fears. Many parents have trouble admitting to their children that they never have had and still don't have all the answers, that sometimes they don't even know the questions. When your young adult returns home, it's important that in the new relationship you include a more realistic picture of who you, the parents, are. The list making we described is an exercise that any family might benefit from, no matter how good they may be at communicating. "I never really knew my parents" can be one of life's great tragedies. Be willing to let youself be known, to say, "I don't like coming home to a dark house at night," or "I sometimes get scared about getting old," or "Listening to a Mahler symphony alone at night in front of the fire fills me with peace."

## Expressing Anger

Figuring out the best way to express anger is where most people get hung up, and you can expect that inevitable angry feelings will be the greatest source of problems you and your son or daughter will have. If you can accept that in the normal course of the homecoming there will be events that make you or your young adult angry, uncomfortable, irritated, upset, furious, provoked, exasperated, disappointed, and frustrated, you will not be caught off guard when these feelings surface. People are entitled to their feelings without shame or guilt or apologies. But they do not have the right to attack or insult the other person with them. Learn to express anger by saying, "I am angry when . . ." without further comment. For example: Martha, forty-seven, a single parent, came home after a ten-hour day in her interior design studio to find that her daughter, Rachel, twenty-six, had not kept one of the bargains she and her mother had made about living together. Martha said, "When I come in tired and in need of some order, and I find the kitchen sink and counters piled with dirty dishes, I feel very angry and even more tired."

This is an appropriate and reasonable way to express anger. A hurtful way to express anger would be if Martha came home and said, "What the hell's wrong with you! Can't you do the few simple things we agreed on? You're so spoiled and thoughtless!" When people are attacked, the normal response is either to withdraw or to counter-attack; the hurtful lashing out can result in days of stony silence or a shouting match. It may be hard to believe that your adult child doesn't know that his or her behavior is annoying, but it can be true. At this particularly difficult time in their lives, returning young adults may be even more self-involved than usual and be less able to think about what other people in the family need and want. The expectation that your adult child should know how you feel isn't a good operating principle here. *Say* what you need and feel, without threatening or attacking, and *before* you feel desperate.

Many people tell us they don't know how to get angry. But anger isn't a skill to be acquired; it is an emotion that we all feel. It's just there. Expressing anger, however, *is* a skill that can be developed. Breaking down the expression of anger into several steps can help you learn to voice anger effectively and calmly, not hurtfully or abusively:

1. Describe what you see (my gas tank is on empty)
2. State the feelings (that's upsetting to me)
3. Say what you need (when you return the car, please fill up the tank)
4. Do not criticize or insult (avoid saying, "You're so damn inconsiderate")

Keep in mind, however, that even after you've made your request, you may not get immediate results. Behavior doesn't change instantly, and you may have to remind your boomerang kid more than once of what you need and expect. If you're patiently treating him or her with goodwill and are working on changing aspects of your behavior that are upsetting to him or her, things will in time begin to work more smoothly.

With adult expectations, you encourage new growth in your young adult children. A sense of responsibility is not something we are born with; living with someone else's house policies and limits is not fun. But life requires both responsibility and accepting limits. It is important to remember what the goal is: to send this young adult forth again a more capable and competent human being.

# FOUR

---

# Mother, Please...
# I'd Rather Do It Myself

## *Respecting the Adult Child*
## *as an Adult*

---

WHEN A YOUNG ADULT in an old television commercial admonished her mother that she wanted to do things her way, telling her in no uncertain terms to butt out, the line "Mother, please — I'd rather do it myself!" struck a universal chord. It touched on a struggle we have all experienced. As adults, we don't want our parents telling us what to do, what to think, or how to be; we want them to bow out unless, of course, we ask for their advice. Just as surely as we want freedom from parental interference in our lives, so do our children want freedom from interference from us.

Undoubtedly, the mother in the commercial who was telling her daughter how to do the laundry was "just trying to help." As parents, we all have only the best of intentions as we tell our adult children how to eat, sleep, dress, think, feel, talk, act, be, what friends to have, whom to sleep with or not sleep with, what job to pursue.

But just what aspects of the young adult's life-style and behavior *are* legitimate concerns of the parents with whom he or she is residing? And which are off limits — none of your business? Trying to decide this may make you feel as though you are threading your way through a mine field.

Respecting your adult children as adults, as separate individual human beings who are entitled to make decisions as to how they will live their lives, is the single most important task to master if you are to move out of old parent-child interactions and build adult-to-adult relationships with your grown children. It's a job so difficult that many parents never quite get there.

One San Diego mother told us, "My daughter had lived on her own for three years after college. I felt I really had been able to relate to her during that time as an adult. I wasn't critical, and I don't think I interfered in her life. But the minute she moved back home for a few months when she was between jobs, I saw my mouth opening and out of it, hanging in the air like words in a comic strip balloon, were things I hadn't said in years . . . 'Where are you going tonight? When will you be home? What do you see in that guy? Why don't you wear your blue dress — it looks so much prettier than the one you have on. I wish you'd cut your hair the way you had it last year. You're eating too much junk food. Are you taking your vitamins?' It was awful, and of course, all we did was fight the whole time she lived at home."

Relating to grown children in a parental way, as this mother did, is so automatic for many parents that they need to make a conscious, deliberate effort to remember what kinds of things are off-limits. Just as your home is your actual physical territory, so too does the boomerang kid have territory — taking "territory" to mean any area of people's lives they feel they own: their home, their ideas, their creative talents, their jobs, their possessions, their psychological space, their financial resources.

Part of the natural response to an invasion of one's territory is to get angry and to defend. We defend when we sense someone is in a place we feel belongs to us. The more something needs protecting, the more we defend. A young adult who has returned home will defend his or her own private territory when parents cross the line.

Fifty-year-old Elinor could not keep any of her opinions to herself about how her twenty-five-year-old daughter, Kara, spent her money. Kara faithfully kept up her end of the bargain that she would pay her mother for room and board. She gave her mother the exact amount promptly every month. But Elinor, who witnessed all the various purchases Kara brought home with her after a shopping trip, was distressed because she thought Kara's purchases were frivolous and unnecessary, and just impulsive spending sprees. The two of them had many words over this, and Kara always ended the exchanges with "It's my money, Mom. I earned it and I can spend it on whatever I want to. I don't tell you how you can spend your money, so don't tell me how to spend mine!" Elinor resolved to keep her mouth shut, but the day Kara told her that she was going to take the entire nest egg she had been saving for a car and invest in a rock band her boyfriend was going to start, Elinor blew up. "You've had some pretty stupid ideas, but this really takes the prize. I don't understand how you can even think of doing such a ridiculous thing. Sam is flaky enough, but the idea that he can make music that anyone would want to listen to is just plain crazy. I don't know what you see in him anyway. I think he just takes advantage of you every chance he gets and . . ."

Kara was furious. She told her mother to stop, that Sam was her business, that her money was her business, and that the whole subject was off-limits.

Kara was defending her territory, and she had every right to do so. Her mother's attacks on her boyfriend and the way she spent her money were intrusions. Had Kara not kept the agreement about the rent, Elinor would have had a right to object in this specific area, but there was nothing in Kara's behavior that had violated their agreement. Elinor was clearly out of bounds. Perhaps investing in the rock band might turn out to be a mistake, and perhaps "flaky" Sam wasn't the best choice for a boyfriend, but these were Kara's decisions to make.

The phrase "I disapprove of what you say, but I will defend to the death your right to say it," attributed to Voltaire, is a good one to keep in mind when trying to honor the autonomy of young adults. Chances are there will be things about the lives and behavior of your grown children that you disapprove of, but as long as they are honoring the agreements they made while living in your home, they have the right to live their lives as they see fit.

## Personal Territory — Keep Out

Here are some general guidelines for territory that should be considered off-limits:

1. Food. Adults have the right to eat what they like, when they want to.
2. Sleep. Adults have the right to sleep as much or as little as they like.
3. Appearance — clothing, hair, makeup, jewelry. Adults have the right to wear whatever clothing, makeup, or jewelry they choose.
4. Friends. Adults have the right to choose their friends.
5. Lovers. Adults have the right to choose their lovers.
6. Jobs. Adults have the right to choose their own job.
7. Money. Adults have the right to spend their money as they choose.

Exceptions occur only when the young adult's exercising of these rights *directly* affects the parents. For example: if your son or daughter is eating a whole week's worth of groceries intended for the entire family, it's time to negotiate. He or she can replace the family groceries, or have a separate food supply on a designated shelf in the refrigerator.

If an adult child comes home noisily at four o'clock in the morning and disturbs the whole family, the issue you have the right to discuss is that the noise has disturbed you — *not* the hours he or she is keeping. If the young adult's appearance constitutes a health hazard (lice, bugs, or dirty clothing that soils the furniture), you have a right to say something about it.

If your adult child's friends disturb you, you have the right to limit the times the friends are in your home — but you have no vote as to the choice of friends. The same is true of lovers.

If your adult child has a job that is illegal, you have a right to say something about that. Buying a young adult a college education, however, does not buy the right to choose the young adult's occupation. The fact that the young adult will work is an appropriate requisite to the return home, but what the young adult does for a living, as long as it is not illegal, is not under your territorial jurisdiction. No matter how embarrassing or demeaning you personally feel the job to be, it is the boomerang kid's business.

If your adult child is spending money and not keeping the financial agreements made with you, you have a right to say something about that, to restate the original agreements. Otherwise, the money is his or hers to spend.

Many of the clashes that occur when the boomerang kid returns home fall into areas that are really a matter of style. Try to let go of having things your way, and recognize that there are *many* "right" ways to do the same thing. Does it matter whether you start slicing a tomato at the stem or at the opposite end? Who cares how the towels are folded? Is it really all that important that the grass trimmer be used before rather than after the lawn is mowed? The boomerang kid didn't come home to learn how to do these kinds of things your way. He or she came home to learn to be independent and self-sufficient, and how the tomatoes are sliced, the towels folded, and all the rest of this small stuff is done has nothing to do with that larger job at hand.

But parents aren't the only ones who intrude into territory where they have no business being. Adult children can get pretty good at that, too. Many adult children think that one manifestation of their own independence and autonomy is the right to declare open season on their parents' life-style, values, and behavior.

Like many boomerang families, Shirlee and Ed, both in their mid-fifties, had filled their empty nest with a busy social calendar that evolved out of many civic activities and club memberships. Although they were members of a local church, they did not attend church regularly, but, as Ed said, "preferred to find God in the woods and mountains" on many of their weekend hikes. They were liberal and open-minded and encouraged their children to develop their own systems of beliefs.

When their oldest son, Fritz, twenty-two, returned home to live after a year abroad traveling with college friends, he brought with him two new passions: a vivacious young woman, Michele, whom he had met in France; and a consuming commitment to a fundamentalist religious group they had both joined in Germany. His parents, although delighted to have Fritz home for a while, were somewhat startled by his unfamiliar religious fervor. He had asked if Michele could stay with the family for several weeks but emphasized that she would have her own room, making a big deal out of the fact that premarital sex was against his beliefs. Right off the bat, Fritz stated that he would like to have a prayer said at the family meals during the time that he was at home. Shirlee and Ed told him that they wouldn't be comfortable with that, but that he could, of course, say a silent prayer if he wanted to. This led to the first of many lectures from Fritz, lectures on his parents' values, morals, and life-style, which all added up to some pretty intense proselytizing. Fritz was judgmental and disapproving of his parents' serving cocktails at a backyard barbecue and of the fact that they didn't own a Bible. His preaching reached a new pitch when he learned that his mother volunteered at a local clinic that provided abortion referrals.

Shirlee and Ed had finally had it. They told their son that they had no objection to his religion. "What you choose to believe is your decision, but what we choose to believe is our decision, and so is how we want to live. This is our home, and we are entitled to make our own choices about what goes on in this home. If you can't stop what you are doing, all this judging and criticizing of the way we live, feel, think, and act, and trying to impose your beliefs on us, then we'll have to ask you to find some other place to live."

Shirlee and Ed's response was a good way to handle this violation of their territory. They were straightforward about their feelings and clear in communicating their expectations, and they consistently voiced these to their son when he continually pushed the limits. Reminding him of the conditions under which he could stay with them left him with the ultimate responsibility of deciding his immediate future.

Because he was a well-intentioned young man, Fritz honored his parents' wishes and learned to keep his differing opinions to himself during the months he stayed in his parents' home. The passion for the young woman he had met in Europe waned with the summer, and along with her went his preoccupation with religion. He felt less critical of his parents as he became involved in job hunting and made several trips out of town for interviews. Leaving

home once again a few months later, Fritz thanked his
parents for "putting up with me last summer."


Another couple felt a similar kind of intrusion when
their twenty-four-year-old daughter came home to live for
a period of time between jobs.

Sally and Dick were both in their late forties; married
in their early twenties, they had a very traditional marriage.
Sally had never worked outside the home, but seemed quite
content with her role of homemaker. She was the daughter
of a controlling and dominating woman who had never
really allowed Sally to grow up. In many ways the dynamics
of Sally's relationship with Dick were similar to the relationship between Sally and her mother. Even at forty-six,
Sally was Dick's "little girl" in many ways. He made most
of the major decisions for the family, and although he was
a loving and kind man, there was clearly a strong parent-
child component to the relationship. But for them it worked
without many major conflicts.

When their daughter Lucy came home, things were initially rather harmonious. Lucy and her mother got along
well together and were pretty good friends. As long as they
stayed on safe subjects, they talked easily and had a good
time together. But Lucy, in trying to carve out her own
identity as a woman, had become very critical of her mother's traditional role, and one evening after dinner she decided to share this opinion with her mother. She told Sally
that she thought she had wasted her life, never developing
any real talent and skills. "You always defer to Dad, and
being handed that allowance he gives you — it's like you're
just a little kid. Do you have any idea how hard it is for
me to try and work out an equal partnership with a man
when all I have for a role model is a mother that acts like

a little girl?" The "discussion" ended with Sally in tears and Lucy lamely apologizing.

Lucy was critical in an area where she had no right to be. Her parents' marriage was not her territory, and she had no right to intrude and force her critical and hurtful observations on her mother. Lucy may have thought that she was being very adult with this "discussion," but she was expressing the hostility of a rebellious adolescent. Lucy wanted a perfect mother she could admire and look up to in all ways; well, she didn't get that. Nobody does! Just as parents often disapprove of aspects of their adult children's lives and behavior, so do children disapprove of their parents. But accepting each other as adult human beings involves giving up the wish for perfection — for perfect parents or perfect children. Being an adult involves forgiveness and acceptance.

## When Territorial Boundaries Are Unclear

Sometimes the boundaries that define territory are fuzzy. "Gretchen and the Case of the Green Hair" was one such situation.

Gretchen was having a hard time getting her life together. Her parents had divorced when she was twelve, and she had bounced back and forth between them for most of her adolescence. After two years of college, during which she barely managed to get passing grades, she dropped out to work, travel, and "find herself." The work was a series of waitress jobs, the last one at a café that catered to artists. Gretchen adapted to the environment at the café in all matters of style, usually wearing flamboyant thrift shop garb and sporting a blond crew cut, from which sprouted one long piece of hair that she had carefully dyed green. When Gretchen got into trouble financially, behind on car payments and on rent, and with three credit cards

over their limits, she asked her dad if she could move home
to save money and get her feet back on the ground. Her
mother, recently remarried, had her hands full with stepchildren, and so her father, who had never remarried, seemed
the logical choice. He loved his daughter but was beginning
to think that because of his guilt over the divorce, he hadn't
expected enough of her, that he had been too easy on her,
not helping her to really mature. She was twenty-five when
she asked to move home again; this time he hoped things
really could be different. He decided he needed some counseling sessions and asked his golf partner, a family prac-
titioner, for the name of a counselor.

With the help of the counselor, Gretchen and her father
were able to negotiate a living arrangement where she par-
ticipated fully in household responsibilities. Together they
also set some achievable financial goals for Gretchen. The
one place they got stuck was around the green hair. "I can't
stand that thing. It looks like a piece of celery sticking out
of her head. If she's going to live with me, it's got to go.
I can't stand being seen with someone who looks like she
belongs in a salad bowl."

Of course, Gretchen responded that it was her hair and
she had a right to have it any color or style that she wished,
and that her dad had no right to dictate to her about it.

The counselor finally got them to agree that Gretchen
had the right to have her hair any way she wanted and
that her father had the right to choose not to take her
places with him, if being with her was embarrassing to
him. It would have been easier if Gretchen's father had
been able to handle Gretchen's hairdo, but he wasn't. He
was a man for whom appearances were very important;
he cared what other people thought of him. The outlandish
green lock in his eyes seemed to be a flag signaling his own
failure as a parent for not raising a "normal" daughter.
He said, "I wouldn't choose friends who looked like that

or want to be with people who looked so weird, so aren't I treating Gretchen as I would any other adult by not wanting to go out in public with her like that?"

As therapists, we had to agree with Gretchen's father, although the sad thing about some conflicts over appearance is that people often deprive themselves of each other's company because of them. However, sometimes, as in this case, the hidden agenda really involved Gretchen's trying to separate from Mom and Dad; green hair (or purple hair or shaved heads or earrings in noses) can be a maneuver to provide some emotional distance for a young adult who fears being helplessly dependent.

## Sex and the Boomerang Kid

One of the areas with the most potential for conflict when the boomerang kid returns home is the delicate subject of sex. The subject ranks right up there with money as one of the most difficult areas for people to talk about, and consequently it is often avoided when the young adult returns home.

Earlier in this chapter, we put the topic of "lovers" on the list of those areas of the young adult's life that were off-limits to parents. Boomerang kids are not children; they are adults. As adults they, and only they, have the right to determine whether they will be sexually active, and homosexual or heterosexual, and whether they will be monogamous or have multiple partners. Issues of sexuality are the personal, private domain of individual adult human beings. Sexuality is an area where parents of adult children have no right to intrude. But the issue of whether or not the boomerang kid is sexually active in your home does fall within your domain, and you do have something to say about it.

In talking with boomerang kids and their families, we

found a wide range of attitudes. Some young adults said it just wasn't an issue that would ever come up. One young man from Boulder who was sharing bachelor quarters with his father told us, "I think that sex was pretty different when my dad was growing up. You didn't do it then as easily because you were afraid of getting a girl in trouble and there wasn't abortion to fall back on. My dad still is kind of hung up on it, I think, but he doesn't say anything about it if I stay out all night. But I'd never think of having sex in his house, I know he couldn't handle it and I'd feel weird, too."

A twenty-two-year-old Salt Lake City student said, "My parents would just get hysterical if they thought I was sexually active. My dad thinks of me as his sweet little girl, and he would probably go after my boyfriend with a flame-thrower if he knew I'm having sex with him. The question of being sexually active while I am living at home is a joke! My folks are not exactly living in the twentieth century."

We also talked with a number of young adults who felt it was their right to have sex while they were living in their parents' home. One Baltimore young woman said, "After I graduated from college, I spent the summer with my boyfriend traveling in Europe. I moved back home when the trip ended, and my boyfriend was going to stay with us for a few days. My mother said we had to have separate rooms. It was ridiculous; I know she knew I'd been sleeping with him. But not only did she say we had to have separate rooms — get this — she said, 'I suppose there will be some bedhopping during the night — but just make sure you end up back in your separate rooms in the morning.' I couldn't believe it. I'm an adult, and of course I'm having sex with him; I thought her deal was so silly and hypocritical."

A Berkeley mother said, "I really tried to be as modern and enlightened as I could when my daughter moved back home. I told her that I would understand if her boyfriend spent the night sometimes. Well, he did spend the night every so often, but then they broke up. Not too long after that, she brought a different guy home to spend the night, and the next week a third guy. I can't tell you how upset I was. My daughter and I had bitter fights about it. She told me I had no right to tell her who she could and couldn't sleep with. I didn't know if I was right or wrong — I only knew I couldn't handle it. I told her from then on as long as she wanted to live under my roof, there would be no overnight guests."

## Sexually Active Single Parents

The difficulty families have with the issue of sexuality isn't always limited to the sexual behavior of the young adults. We talked with a number of sexually active single parents who experienced difficulties themselves once their adult children returned home.

"My sexual freedom ended when my son came back home eight months ago," a forty-six-year-old Seattle mother lamented. "I got married at eighteen to the first boy I ever had sex with, and I always felt I missed out on all the experiences that everyone else seemed to be having. So when my husband died three years ago and I started dating again, I thought I'd see what this was all about. I found out that I wasn't cut out for casual sex, but I began seeing one man steadily and we began sleeping together. I don't want to marry again right away, but I do care for him and I enjoy our sex life. When my son needed my help again, that all went out the window. The man I've been seeing has a teenaged daughter still at home with him, and we have no place to go now. This is part of the resentment I feel toward my son's being back home with me. Being in bed with a man and having my son in the next room just isn't something I could do."

A single father in his fifties told us that when he brought a woman home to spend the night, his adult son found it very upsetting. "He actually told me he thought that parents only did it for breeding purposes!" the father said.

In contrast to this father and son, we talked with another single father, living in a small apartment, who said he and his son had tried to work out an arrangement a lot like college roommates in coed dorms do, where they signal each other if one of them has a woman in the room. "Do you remember that the reporter for the *Washington Post* who was investigating the Watergate scandal used to signal his government source that he wanted to see him by putting a red flag in a flowerpot on his apartment balcony?" asked the Chicago father. "Well, when my son came back to live with me, we had to work out a system that said we didn't want to see each other, and boy, sometimes it was pretty trying. I'd turn into the driveway after a long day at the office and see that damn red flag in the planter by the garage, and know I was supposed to keep on driving. You better believe we eventually worked out a better deal. I hadn't counted on losing control of my home, you know."

The word *hypocritical* came up over and over again when we talked with boomerang families about sex. One single mother told us she felt hypocritical telling her twenty-three-year-old daughter who was living with her that she couldn't have her boyfriend spend the night, when she herself allowed a man she dated steadily to stay over on weekends when her daughter was out of town. "I keep telling myself that it's my house and I can do what I want, but I feel like I'm talking out of both sides of my mouth. I always felt stupid saying 'do as I say, not as I do' and this sure sounds like that, but I'm just too uncomfortable with Jinny and her boyfriend making love down the hall from me, and I guess she'll just have to live with that if she wants to live with me."

## Honoring Your Need for Emotional Comfort

Even though the young adult's sexuality is not your business, your emotional comfort is your business and the boomerang kid needs to respect that. Because you are parent and child, sexual issues are often the most difficult to talk about. We are sexual beings, but because of universal prohibitions against incest, we do our best to repress our sexual feelings for family members who are not our mates. We may feel some discomfort that we don't fully understand. We often find it disturbing to know our adult child is making love in the next room. This is only human. Try to accept that at times you will feel uncomfortable, inconsistent, illogical, or hypocritical when you are confronted with the idea of your adult child's sexual activity. You are entitled to emotional comfort in your own home, and to protect that comfort by setting house policies.

Parents who intellectually don't disapprove of premarital sex may still have some anxious thoughts about having a sexually active adult child at home. Middle-aged parents of boomerang kids have had to endure dramatic social change that has put more stress on the family institution than in any other period in American history. Try to appreciate how much you've had to adapt to. Emotionally you may carry a large residue of your own rigid programming about sexuality; many parents just can't gracefully adapt to today's mores. If your adult child cannot learn to be sensitive to your emotional discomfort and respect your right to determine a policy regarding overnight guests in your own home, then perhaps he or she will need to face the consequences of living independently without your help.

## Sex and the Need for Privacy

For those parents who can accept their adult child's being sexually active at home, scheduling may help avoid embarrassing and uncomfortable situations. If space is limited and privacy hard to find, being flexible and considerate eases the problem. For example, you may agree to be away from your home for a prearranged amount of time. In one family, when her daughter asked if she could be alone in the apartment with her boyfriend, Diane, a single parent, made plans with a friend to be away until midnight. Diane was sensitive to her daughter's need for privacy and didn't feel as if she was being displaced. Her daughter, too, made arrangements to be elsewhere on some occasions so that Diane could have privacy.

All parents, not just sexually active single parents, have every right to ask their adult child to be away from their home. Keep in mind, however, that you have agreed to let your adult child make this temporarily his or her home also, and asking him or her to leave too often may not only be disruptive, but feel like rejection.

# FIVE

---

# And Baby Makes Three

*Special Issues in the
Three-Generational Household*

---

THREE GENERATIONS under one roof can triple the pleasure, triple the fun, and sometimes . . . triple the trouble. Although the joys of grandparenting are many, when a daughter (or sometimes a son) boomerangs home with a child there are many additional problems to be solved. And in today's world, where most households aren't set up for more than two generations, the problems can seem overwhelming.

In the past, young people used to be able to turn to parents and grandparents for help and support in the daily rearing of their children. Older generations fully expected to participate in family responsibilities well into their old age. But today, while there are still people who live and die within a twenty-mile radius of where they were born, many of us are now several hours by plane from our nearest relatives.

Consequently, when today's boomerang kid comes home with a baby, it's a whole new ball game. Often not yet ready for the role of grandparent, Mother and Dad have looked forward to their empty nest, usually with the thought that their personal sacrifices for the care, feeding, and education of their children were behind them. They anticipated a life-style in their middle years that (with the exceptions of weekend, summer, or holiday visits) did not include helping with changing diapers, cleaning sticky fingerprints off the new dining room wallpaper, and listening to cries and shrieks of infants.

Few experiences have so much potential for joy, but also for conflict, as helping a young family get back on its feet. In raising children, parents must nurture, nourish, take care of, provide for, and protect. A parent also teaches, sets limits, disciplines, guides, directs, shapes, molds, and models. However, as we've already pointed out, the adult child who comes home isn't a child anymore. Some parents can't figure that out and continue to tell their grown children what to do, when to do it, and even how to do it. Quite naturally, the adult child rebels against this intrusion into his or her life. When adult children are also parents themselves, they feel a fierce need to protect their right to choose how they will parent and to resist any attempted takeovers by the grandparents. The return home challenges this important piece of identity. Both sides need to acknowledge the stress that will be put on their relationship, but here there are other potential difficulties that will affect all three generations.

Some grandparents try a "hands-off" policy, completely staying out of the relationship between the boomerang kid and his or her child — but it usually doesn't work. They usually find they cannot stay out of child-care issues for long when confronted with them on a daily basis, as they inevitably will be. To ensure peace and harmony, the three-generational family needs to work out a system that respects the autonomy of the young adult parent, meets the best interest of the child, and recognizes the role of the grandparents.

## A Model for Letting Go

One grandmother's handling of the situation stands out as a model for coping with it with maturity and compassion. Her daughter, Jillian, twenty-nine, belonged to the new breed of superwomen. Bright and aggressive, Jillian completed her master's degree a year after finishing college, and quickly began her five-, ten-, and fifteen-year plans to climb fast and high in a commercial real estate company with national offices. Not in the plan, but seemingly taken in stride, came marriage and, less than a year later, a baby boy, Matthew. Friends marveled at how effortlessly Jillian seemed to march toward her goals, hiring household help and day care for the baby, entertaining her and her husband's business associates in their attractively furnished townhouse, and achieving an enviable record of sales closings. No one seemed to notice that her already slim figure was getting thinner, but close friends did notice that she had begun smoking again and was not as relaxing to be around. She did not share with even her best friend that she and her husband had begun to quarrel frequently over her suspicions that he was having an affair.

Although Jillian's pace in the office never let up, at home things were crumbling under her feet. When Matthew was four and a half, she and her husband separated, and divorced a year later after a lengthy battle over custody and property. The first signs of Jillian's depression emerged as a mild sleep disturbance and some inability to remember details of her crowded life, but Jillian still managed to keep both her work world and her home life reasonably on track most of the time. The turning point came when Jillian's housekeeper, who was Matthew's principal caretaker, decided to return to her native Sweden, and Jillian was unable to find a replacement. Although Matthew was now in first grade, the housekeeper had cared for him before school, after school, and into many evenings when Jillian's work demanded extra social activities. Caught between the pressures of a job where she felt she had to perform beyond anyone's expectations and her responsibility for her son, whose twenty-four-hour care presented her with a seemingly insoluble problem, Jillian fell apart.

Her mother flew from her home five hundred miles away to pick up Matthew after Jillian's best friend called her to say that Jillian had been taken to the psychiatric ward of a nearby hospital the night before. Three weeks later, Jillian was released from the hospital; emotionally and physically exhausted, she joined her son at her parents' home. Matthew, who had abruptly been taken away from all his familiar faces, became a frightened, confused, and tearful little boy. When his mother arrived, he rejected his grandmother's attention and clung wordlessly to Jillian, although she was unable to meet any of his needs.

Her young grandson's distress added significantly to the weight Jillian's mother carried. Not only did she bear the burden of Jillian's illness, returning to a caretaking role for her daughter, but she assumed a parenting role with Matthew. Reluctantly and slowly, Matthew allowed his grandmother to take his mother's place in meeting his needs. Although his grandmother had a good deal of compassion and understanding for the losses and adjustment difficulties Matthew was struggling with, she was able to maintain a firm, consistent pattern of discipline with him, expecting him to behave in a manner that was appropriate for a six-year-old. She was able, gently but firmly, to weather the storm when Matthew would shout at her, "You're not my mother! I don't have to listen to you."

As the weeks passed, however, he found comfort in her loving, if sometimes frustrated, attempts to make him feel secure, and he silently slid into turning to her more and more for his emotional and physical needs. While Jillian slowly returned to health, Matthew almost completely shifted his requirements for mothering to his grandmother.

Jillian's inner resources were gradually strengthened by months in the supportive environment of her family and by the progress she was making in psychotherapy. As her capacity to deal with the demands of life increased, she began to take back responsibility for her son with some of the same driven quality with which she had approached her life previously. But Matthew, who sought out his grandmother upon his return from school each day to share drawings and papers with her over cookies and juice, did not easily shift his attention back to Jillian.

Within a short time Jillian began to feel anger and resentment toward both her mother and her son. She was jealous of their relationship, aware that once again Matthew had someone other than her as his primary attachment, a pattern she now wanted to change. Jillian's mother understood her daughter's feelings, but she had difficulty giving up a relationship that had worked in the best interest of her grandson and been very satisfying to her.

She discussed the dilemma with her husband, a quiet man who was supportive but had remained very much in the background. She reminded herself that the first goal had been to provide Matthew with a safe haven while Jillian regained her health. "I think I've done pretty well with that. But I know I have to help Matthew make another change. He can do it, too — he's quite a kid. When I think that he lost his father, his nanny, his school friends, his playmates, and his mother all at once and yet how well he's doing now — laughing a lot, playing jokes on us, and doing pretty well in school — well, I know that it's time for me to ease out of the picture. Jillian has a right to be a mother again."

Jillian's mother started by deciding not to be home every afternoon when Matthew returned from school. Although at first he called for his grandmother, in time he began to greet his mother just as eagerly. His grandmother increasingly told him to "ask your mother" when he would request permission to do something, which helped Matthew accept Jillian's parental role once again. And she increasingly used the phrase "your mother and I think . . ." or "your mother and I feel that . . ." to reinforce his mother's role in his life.

By the end of the following summer, nearly two and a half years after her depression began, Jillian and Matthew moved into their own home about six blocks away. Jillian returned to work in a less demanding job that gave her more time for Matthew, whom she dropped off and picked up before and after school at her parents' home. Jillian's mother loved her ongoing relationship with Matthew for those few hours each day, but it was clear that Jillian was his mother.

This family had successfully weathered the kind of storm that in other families has caused irreparable damage to those involved.

The key was that throughout the crisis Jillian's mother was able to remember what the long-range goal was: helping Jillian regain her independence — and what the immediate task was: providing security for Matthew during this period. She recognized her daughter's right to be a mother to her own son as Jillian became progressively able to resume that role, and she thought of ways she could actively ease Jillian's transition from dependency to autonomy. Jillian's mother loved taking care of her grandson, but she still was able to help Matthew transfer his primary attachment back to his mother as Jillian became stronger; by gradually removing herself, she helped Matthew turn to his mother for support and direction. Jillian's mother never forgot whose child he was.

*IT'S HER/HIS CHILD* should be your first guiding principle when young adults, no matter what shape they might be in, return home with a child. But often this principle may seem to run counter to the fact that *IT'S YOUR HOUSE*, which we suggested in chapter three. And that's where so many three-generational families get into trouble.

## Working as a Team

Conflict erupted when Jan, twenty-seven, returned to her mother's home with her four-year-old daughter, Erica. Jan had been divorced when Erica was two and had worked at a travel company specializing in tour packages. When the company had to drastically cut its staff, Jan was laid off. She asked to live with her parents until she could find another job. In the years since her divorce, Jan had lived with a series of roommates, both male and female, none of whom seemed to work out. When they left they usually complained that they just couldn't deal with Erica's behavior. Erica was an energetic and intelligent child, but Jan's inability to set limits and discipline Erica created a real problem. It was a problem that became painfully clear to Jan's mother, Helen, as soon as Jan and Erica moved in.

Helen, sixty-two, was a retired schoolteacher. She was a strict, authoritarian woman, both in raising her own children and in her classroom. She believed she had survived years of coping with the discipline problems of other people's children because she had been such a strict disciplinarian, setting out her classroom rules clearly on the first day every fall and expecting them to be followed, no ifs, ands, or buts about it. She was enormously frustrated with Erica, who just seemed to run wild.

In raising Erica, Jan had not wanted to duplicate her own strict upbringing. She tried to give her little daughter reasons and elaborate explanations: "Erica, we don't want you to tip over the plant because it's not good for the plant to be tipped over and then we'll have to clean up all the dirt from the floor," she would reason, instead of simply saying "no." Jan wanted to encourage her child's natural inquisitiveness, and she thought of most discipline as oppressive. Erica could reach the refrigerator door and was in and out of it all day, taking any food she could reach and eating it all over the house. She climbed all over the furniture, turned the television on and off, and fiddled with the knobs on the stereo system. At every turn, Helen was yelling, "Erica, *no!*" to the child, and Jan was saying, "Oh, Mother, she's not really hurting anything."

Helen was a collector of hand-blown glass, much of which she and her husband had accumulated over the years on various trips. The tables in the living room were filled with all kinds of knickknacks, and the curio cabinet in the dining room held cranberry glass and a collection of glass animals. Jan tried to keep Erica away from her mother's fragile possessions by distracting her with toys and coloring books, but the temptations were too much for the little girl. Her grandfather, who usually left the child care to the women, got into the act one evening after dinner when Jan and her mother were cleaning up in the kitchen. He yelled at Erica to keep out of the curio cabinet, but it was too late. A piece of valuable glass was irreparably broken. When Helen saw the broken glass, she burst into tears of anger and frustration. This set off her husband, who gave Erica a good whack on the bottom. "Don't you ever hit my child!" Jan screamed at her father, who bellowed back, "This is my house!"

After that, the tension in the house became unbearable, and in desperation Helen called the counselor at the school where she had taught. The counselor recommended seeing a family therapist, and Helen helped her husband and her daughter to see that they could all use some help. Everyone agreed to give it a try.

Usually when a couple or a family goes for counseling, each person has the secret hope that the therapist will magically "fix" the others. That's what Jan and her parents were each hoping. Each side wanted the therapist to declare his or her position right. In the initial sessions, when the battle lines emerged as the old "It's my house" and "It's my child" conflict, the therapist told them that they were *each* right. The grandparents did have something to say about their territory; and Jan, the parent, did have something to say about how her child would be treated. But to find a workable solution, they would have to give. "It's our house" was modified to "It's our house, but we must adjust to the needs of a child," while the statement "It's my child" was broadened to "It's my child, but my child must learn to live in the home of other adults." There was nothing new in this thinking, but, as in so many cases, it took a third party to help the family see the problem more objectively, ease away from two rigid stances toward a middle ground, and begin to find a solution.

The first concrete thing the family worked out with the therapist's help was that the house needed to be child-proofed. It was unrealistic to think that a four-year-old who had never experienced any kind of limit could suddenly be expected not to touch intriguing and breakable objects that were within easy reach. The grandparents were the first ones to give. They found it easier to accept this suggestion from the therapist than when their daughter had insisted on it. They agreed to get all the breakable items out of the way, and to fill the lower shelves of the curio cabinet with little stuffed animals that Erica could play with. In turn, Jan agreed that the television and the stereo would always be off-limits to Erica, and that she would be allowed to eat only in the kitchen.

Once the family had agreed on territorial ground rules, they moved on to the touchy area of discipline. The therapist, who discovered Jan's father was an avid sports fan, offered the concept of coaching, with Jan as Erica's head coach. The rules pertaining to Erica's meals, nap, bedtime, and behavior were to be set by Jan. The grandparents would serve as assistant coaches who, as Jan wished, agreed never to hit the child, but were to back up Jan on the system she designed. As head coach, she was to take into account the needs of the grandparents as one of her responsibilities. The therapist helped Jan create a system of "time-outs" for Erica if she had temper tantrums or didn't respect the house rules. These were times when she had to stay in her room alone until she thought she could control herself. With the therapist, Jan devised a reward system of gold stars to reinforce Erica's good behavior. Each member of the "coaching staff" gave out the stars, and the stars could earn trips to the zoo with Grandpa and making a cake with Grandma.

The family met with the therapist for three more sessions in which they reviewed the system and made adjustments. For example, Jan's flexible nap schedule for Erica had created problems for the grandparents, who were bothered by the noise of Erica's staying up long after they were in bed. Jan agreed to try a fixed nap schedule. The therapist stressed that there would never be a perfect system or a conflict-free household, and helped them create realistic expectations of the process they were trying to initiate. Within their meetings the most important thing had happened. They were talking to each other, trying to respect each other's feelings, and each side was giving. When that happens, even though there will always be skirmishes, the battle is mostly over.

Under stress even the most sensible people tend to insist on their own ideas of right or wrong, which are often merely disguises for getting their own way. Sometimes a third party can help them create a structure where they begin to think less rigidly and can move on to solving the problems. Jan and her parents were fortunate to have the ingredients necessary for success. They all *wanted* it to work, and they all had the maturity to compromise and give. No one *had* to be "right." One of the best outcomes of the situation was that Erica was able to know her grandparents in a new way. Before the "coaching staff" got it together, Erica's grandparents seemed to her to be just mean people who yelled at her for everything. In fact, so much of their energy had gone into telling her "No!" and "Don't touch!" that she never went to them for anything playful and happy. But after this change in their approach, Jan often found Erica curled up in Grandpa's lap hearing a story or telling Grandma about the adventures of Floppy, Erica's favorite stuffed rabbit. When Jan moved into her own home again, her parents were grateful for peace and privacy again but missed what she and Erica had added to their lives.

## Emotional Territory

Even when two generations can come together to set house rules, develop a similar parenting style, and reach a mutual understanding of the child's needs, they will still find large, gray areas of confusion where conflict can arise — areas in which again "It's our house" clashes head-on with "It's my child." We've talked a lot about territory in previous chapters; it's in the area of emotional territory — your feelings and what you're comfortable with — that so many of these conflicts flare up.

Emotional territory is often violated when divorced adult children bring conflict with former spouses into their parents' home. As we all know, the conflicts of a troubled marriage don't always end with the divorce. Former spouses continue to interact angrily and often use their children to get at each other. Divorce ends marriage; it doesn't end relationships or families. And there are all sorts of events that force the formerly marrieds and in-laws to relate to each other. When a divorced couple continues to reenact old battles, life is difficult enough for the children; but when they extend the battleground to the grandparents' home, they bring misery where it doesn't belong. Sometimes the only solution is to tell the no-longer-marrieds to take their fight elsewhere.

It was partially this violation of emotional territory that led fifty-six-year-old Joe of Salt Lake City to explode. Joe and his wife, Mary, agreed to let their twenty-five-year-old daughter, Kim, and her two daughters, five years and eighteen months, live with them while Kim looked for a new house. Kim had undergone a messy divorce; she and her ex-husband were fiery foes who could not even discuss the weather without a fight. Their six-year marriage had been one long battle, and it didn't end with the divorce. Not only did Joe and Mary find themselves trying to adapt to three new members of their household, but they were faced with angry phone calls and weekend confrontations when their former son-in-law came to see the children. Their once peaceful home had become a war zone, and they felt helpless as they watched their daughter and her ex-husband continue to point blaming fingers at each other and use their five-year-old daughter to communicate their anger to each other. Joe would overhear Kim tell the child, "Ask your father why he can't manage to keep his promises and get you back on time." And the child reported that her father told her to "tell your mother it really fries me that she can't take better care of the clothes I buy you." The little girl became increasingly jittery as each weekend approached, responding to the stress by wetting the bed on the nights following her father's visits.

Joe became increasingly fed up with the situation, and

tried to get his wife to do something about it. "It's a mother's place to talk to her daughter about these things. This situation stinks!" Mary complained that Kim wouldn't listen to her, and then harped on the fact that she thought Kim should never have married the guy in the first place. Neither of the grandparents knew what to do, and Mary became distant toward her former son-in-law when he came to pick up the children. She was polite, but cool. Joe had usually tried to make sure he wasn't around during these encounters, but he still felt drawn into it. When the child returned quite upset after one weekend and told the family that her father said for "me to tell Gramma to stop being mean to Daddy," Kim retaliated by calling her ex-husband and screaming, "You get the kids so stirred up! I'll stop you from seeing them at all — even if I have to go back to court!"

The next time the children's father came to pick them up and the fighting began again, Joe confronted both the young parents about "this ridiculous situation you put us all through." His voice shaking with rage, he added, "I don't know what to do about this, but I can't stand what's happening here. Mostly I can't stand what's happening to my grandchildren. I'm mad at myself for waiting so long to tell you two to quit it. I'm angry at my wife for not being able to do what I couldn't do myself. And I'm furious with both of you for bringing this outrage into my home. You two can fight all you want to, but it's not *my* fight and I won't have it in my house. Take it out of here, and leave my granddaughters out of it while you're at it!"

Although the intervention was late and came out with volcanic force, Joe did regain control of his emotional territory, the comfort and peaceful environment he wished to live in. Having reached the end of his patience with the young parents, he set limits on what they could do in his house.

This family had no idea of how to deal with conflict, but Joe's demand that the open hostilities end had an effect on everyone. Sometimes people are immobilized in hostile situations because they feel they need to have a solution all worked out before they do anything at all. This can be a barrier to change. However, you can just stop doing whatever you are doing — nothing more. This in itself is a change. When the unproductive behavior ceases, emotional comfort gradually returns and some space is created for finding successful solutions. Joe did know enough to say "Enough already!"

Mary was strengthened by her husband's firm stand and made an effort to be more cordial to her former son-in-law. She told him she appreciated his continuing interest in the kids. As she softened, he began to feel less as if he were entering enemy territory. Both the young parents made efforts to be polite to each other and keep the kids out of it. The children's play began to reflect less of the aggressive quarreling that had mirrored their parents' style. The parents never reached a really good working arrangement, but they did stop using the kids to get at one another.

Joe's emotional territory had been violated by the fighting in his house. His home life was being disrupted, and he had a right to call a halt to it. He also had a right to intervene because his granddaughter was obviously upset and hurt by the emotionally abusive situation. You need to intervene when the welfare, safety, or emotional well-being of children is at stake, or if the young adult parents are neglecting or abusing their child.

It's important, however, that grandparents not use this principle as an excuse to intrude into areas of child care where they don't belong. Ask yourself whether you're using the "My grandchild is getting hurt" criterion as a rationale for imposing your own pet child-care notions on the young adult parent. The statements "I have to stop this behavior because it's hurting my grandchild to eat between meals," "to watch cartoons," "to eat so much candy," "to play with toy guns," "to wear that dirty shirt," all fall into areas where grandparents don't belong. Although it may be true that the child would be better off if he or she didn't have snacks, candy, or toy guns or watch a lot of television, the grandparent must respect the autonomy of the young adult parent to decide these issues. Even if some of these things drive you crazy, remember that you had your turn at being parents; now your young adult child deserves hers or his.

## Flexibility and Sensitivity

Most of the three-generational households that achieve a reasonable degree of harmony have adult members who are flexible and sensitive to each other's feelings. This was the case when Daniel, twenty-six, became the sole parent of his two-year-old son, Brandon, after his wife, Sandra, died following a long hospitalization after a car accident. Financially depleted by child-care costs and hospital bills, Daniel and his son moved in with his fifty-two-year-old mother, Natalie, in her home in Chicago.

Natalie was happy to be able to help them, and looked forward to having her grandson around. The move was a drastic change for Brandon, who was not only going through the "terrible twos" but feeling, as they all were, the tragic loss of his mother.

When they first moved in, Brandon did not seem to mind his father's morning departure for work, but when Daniel returned home he would cling to him, refusing to let his grandmother near him. Natalie would offer her grandson candy if he would come to her, and when Daniel would object not only to the bribe but also to the candy before dinner, Natalie would say, "I'm only trying to help."

Brandon's anxiety began to include a refusal to go to bed without his father sitting by the crib. When Natalie tried to intervene, suggesting that Daniel allow his son to stay up a while, Daniel snapped, "Mom, stay out of this." Natalie retreated, feeling upset.

A pattern developed where Natalie would parent Brandon as she thought best during the day, only to have Daniel come home at night and present the little boy with a different set of expectations, insisting that Natalie remain silent. Natalie finally confronted Daniel: "We've got a problem here. I try to be Brandon's mother and grandmother all day, which is hard enough. But you've got these strong ideas about how this ought to be done, and, even more, how I should do it. That gets very obvious when you come in at night. I can't just be a carbon copy of your style any more than you can of mine, and I can't make a fast switch from making minute-by-minute decisions about Brandon to turning that all over to you as soon as you come home. I feel criticized constantly. That's just too hard for me, and I don't think either of us thought it would be this way. I need, and certainly Brandon needs, for us to figure out what to do about this now."

At first Daniel insisted that he was the father and he was going to raise his son the way he wanted, and the way he knew Sandra would have wanted. He went on to complain that his mother gave in to Brandon too often and that she was spoiling him. The discussion would have ended in a stalemate, but Natalie declined to debate her son. Instead, she restated her frustration with the situation, adding, "You know, Dan, it would be different if Brandon were just visiting. It used to be easy when you and Sandra would come for the holidays. I liked spoiling him; that's what grandmothers are for. But today I don't think letting him have his way in little things is spoiling him. I do think a great deal about what I am doing; I'm just trying not to be too hard on a little boy who has had a lot of loss in his short life."

Over the next few days, Daniel began slowly to realize that he had been asking too much of his mother, who really was trying hard to do what he had actually asked her to. He recognized what a bind he had put his mother and son in, by expecting the fast switch of both of them, and finally was able to see his demands as unreasonable. Toward the end of the week he said, "Mom, I don't know what to do, but I'm willing to talk about this and work something out with you. I'm just mixed up about how I fit into Brandon's life without Sandra, and when I don't do things exactly the way I think she would have done them, I feel I'm letting her down."

Natalie and Daniel spent some time over the following evenings talking about what they could do together to share the parenting of Brandon. Their final agreement included ideas from both of them so that each was satisfied with the outcome. When Sandra was alive, she and Daniel had taken a Parent Effectiveness Training class. Daniel asked his mother if she would take the class with him now at the community college. Natalie agreed, and in turn asked Daniel if he would be willing to read a book she had read and found helpful in understanding what Brandon might be going through. Daniel agreed, saying, "I guess I need all the help I can get."

Daniel and Natalie finally reached a place where they could each let go and give something to each other. Solutions cannot be reached without this: developing the ability to let go.

Natalie's initial confrontation with her son was productive because of Natalie's refusal to be drawn into an argument and get sidetracked by other issues. Instead of arguing about the "right" way to handle Brandon, she repeated and stayed with her observation that what they were doing wasn't working for either of them, and certainly not for Brandon, and that they needed to find a better way. And she added her willingness to work together with her son in establishing co-territory they could manage jointly.

Daniel was struggling with some crucial changes and important losses when he returned home to live with his mother. Natalie was wise enough to tell her son she knew these were hard for him, a message he finally heard as he felt her compassion for his distress. This recognition paved the way for Daniel's willingness to seek a compromise that involved his letting go of territory he had felt was solely his.

Flexibility and letting go, however, are not easily acquired, and sometimes the situation is totally unworkable. Sadly, there are times when families cannot and do not work through their relationships. Sometimes it is just too hard for parents, given their individual histories, to accept the individuality and differences in their adult children. Their children's life-styles violate their own values, or are simply outside their own experience and they cannot accept something they do not understand. Further, their thinking does not include asking for outside help, and they get stuck in a battle between "right" and "wrong." The unhappy ending is the withdrawal of both sides into their separate worlds again.

Peg and Bert lived in a town of 18,000. It was a farming community with deeply religious roots, in which Bert owned the hardware store and Peg gave piano lessons from their Victorian home. Shari, twenty, was their only child, and they had doted on her most of her life. Shari was a nice-looking, pleasant young woman who had been a princess in the town Strawberry Festival. The family was active in the town; Bert had twice been president of Rotary, and they were pillars of the Methodist church where Bert was a deacon and Peg sang in the choir. They had planned and saved carefully for Shari's college education at the state university 250 miles away.

What they hadn't planned on was Shari's pregnancy during her sophomore year. Shari had been raised with strong antiabortion sentiments. When she announced to her boyfriend her intention of having and keeping the baby, he told her he didn't want any part of it. She kept the news of her pregnancy from her parents until she was in her eighth month, when she tearfully called her mother. Peg was furious and ashamed. All she could say was "How could you do this to me!" Shari's father was equally upset, but he was able to tell Shari to come home.

After the baby was born, Peg was so embarrassed by what she considered to be a real skeleton in the family closet that she seldom went into town. Nor did she want Shari being seen there with the baby. Shari, feeling guilty and dependent, complied on the surface with her mother's demands. She had always been an obedient child, eager to please her parents, but the anger she felt stayed bottled up inside.

As the baby grew and changed, Peg was unable to take any pleasure in her grandchild. Instead, she daily criticized the way Shari was taking care of the baby, rarely offering to help with the child herself. Even though the baby seemed secure and content, Shari's self-esteem and confidence were shaken by her mother's constant attacks. Bert was able to take more of an interest in the baby than was his wife, and Peg angrily accused him of encouraging Shari to "just go out and do it again." They had fight after angry fight, and finally Bert began sleeping in a separate bedroom.

When the baby was six months old, Bert gave Shari a job in his hardware store. Even though many people in the community knew about Shari's baby, and many weren't nearly as judgmental as Peg thought, Peg didn't want a sitter in the house who might "tell our business to the whole town." So Peg took over the baby's daytime care. When Shari came home from work with her father, Peg now complained of physical and emotional exhaustion from "having to take care of that baby."

The situation was becoming intolerable for Shari; but until she could save enough money she felt helpless, totally dependent on her parents, and particularly unable to defend herself and stand up to her mother. Bert silently sided with his daughter, and secretly gave her money to add to her savings for her move out of the home so she could resume working and going to school. When the baby was eight months old, Shari did move out. Except for occasional phone conversations with her father, Shari broke off virtually all contact with her parents. At Christmas when she called to ask how Shari was, Peg wasn't able to keep from making references to Shari's "past sins."

Shari, whose self-regard had been bolstered with the help of a campus therapist, said, "You have a real problem, Mother. I'm not a bad person. I may have made a mistake, but I will not pay for it in your eyes the rest of my life."

In the infrequent contact they had, Shari continually refused to put up with her mother's verbal abuse. The realization that she was actually losing her daughter eventually moved Peg toward a less rigid stance, and she finally invited Shari to bring the baby home for his first birthday.

Peg's attitudes and her initial inability to come to terms with her daughter's situation may seem to some a bit of an anachronism, given the number of teenage pregnancies today. Although her feelings seem extreme, many middle-aged parents have a great deal of difficulty in coping with a young adult daughter who chooses to have a baby without a husband. Their sense of shame and disappointment often makes it difficult for them to meet the needs of their boomerang kid. One needs the capacity to set aside his or her own feelings in order to give the young adult the support and caring she needs to begin a new life with a baby and without a partner; yet sometimes, as in Peg's case, that's too much for parents. Given Peg, Bert, and Shari's limited emotional resources for dealing with the crisis that had entered their lives, they had few options. Parents can accept the mistakes and poor judgment or differing values of their children only if they have learned to forgive their own shortcomings first. Peg's rigid moral code initially kept her from such forgiveness, and her shaky sense of self-worth, apparent in her excessive concern for the approval of others, certainly added to her inability to take a less harsh position with her daughter.

## *The Need for Privacy*

Most three-generational families *can* find a workable solution. In those who were the most successful we found another important common ingredient: they gave each other some time for privacy and solitude. We all have different needs in this regard, but all of us need a place where we can be by ourselves when we want to be. Children will stretch a blanket across chairs and hide inside to play, or when they are older construct a clubhouse in the backyard where they can retreat. One of our daughters posted a warning sign on her bedroom door when she was seven — "Nock Before Nter" — letting us all know she wanted privacy. Adolescents put on earphones to listen to their music but also to be alone in that world. Some can find private space in a city park in the middle of honking horns while others hike miles into the wilderness before they find the solitary place they need. But everyone needs privacy at some time or other.

The families who worked particularly well together were able to plan times when the young adult parent and the grandchildren would be away for the day or the evening to give the grandparents some privacy and solitude. And the grandparents often took the children out to give the young parent some private time and emotional space.

When a boomerang kid returns with a grandchild, we suggest following the guidelines in chapter three, "No Free Lunch," to help the young adult parent become independent as soon as possible. But, in addition, we recommend setting house policies that include the needs of small children, and applying the "coaching staff" concept to the issues of child care, with the young adult parent functioning as the head coach. And when the principle of "It's our house" collides with "It's my child," as it often does, remember that the families who work their way through the conflict successfully are those who bend a little this way, a little that.

Legend says that the Chinese symbol for "trouble" shows two women standing under the same roof. It's important not to underestimate the potential for conflict in the three-generational household. But for those parents who have the sensitivity and flexibility to make it work, it can be a special time for them to know and love their grandchildren. The opportunity to live with a grandchild, giving care and love on a daily basis, can provide the foundation for a very precious relationship.

# SIX

# When Love Isn't Enough

*Seeking Professional Help*

SOMETIMES THE LOVE parents have for their children isn't enough. Sometimes constructive, purposeful parental support to encourage eventual independence again, and all the understanding and empathy the family can muster, simply aren't adequate. Certain young adults need more than their parents can offer. They need professional help.

"We tried everything," the mother of a seriously depressed twenty-two-year-old son told us, "but nothing worked. We talked everything over when he first moved back home, from how long he planned to be here to how we would work out all the details of living, the stereo, the phone, grocery shopping, and especially what kinds of things he'd do for us instead of paying rent. We clearly stated our expectations of him and yet, at the same time, I think we made every effort to understand what he was going through. We knew it was hard for John, having lost his job, but he just seemed to go downhill. He couldn't get anything done and began sleeping most of the day. He looked terrible, and seemed to stop taking care of himself. His father and I didn't know what to do."

*Love Is Not Enough,* the title of Dr. Bruno Bettelheim's

landmark book on the treatment of emotionally disturbed children, discusses the need for professional help in caring for these children. His phrase "Love is not enough," written well over thirty years ago, contains an important message to parents today confronted with adult children who need help beyond what the family can provide.

How do you know if you can't do it yourself, and need professional help? Many parents don't know what the signs are, or when they do suspect that something is wrong, they tend to look the other way. Understandably, they find the idea that their child may be in serious emotional trouble tough to swallow. Acknowledging that someone you love is having psychiatric problems is painful. As parents, we want to believe that our child is really okay for his or her sake, and for our sake as well. If our children are having serious problems, we worry that there may have been something terribly wrong with our parenting. We are threatened by the possibility of our own failure.

## Clinical Depression

Most people experience variations in mood, a range of ups and downs — the "blues," the "blahs," and times of feeling sad. Sadness is a normal emotion, and a healthy response to a loss; it is not a disease. The medical and psychological disorder called depression goes beyond sadness or the "blues"; yet, because it resembles these normal emotions, clinical depression can be especially difficult for the average person to recognize. We often make the mistake of thinking that clinically depressed people are just feeling sorry for themselves, that they're lacking moral character or the fortitude to pull themselves up by their bootstraps. It rarely occurs to us that something physiological may be going on, something over which they may have little control. We have difficulty recognizing that the person is as ill, and as much in need of help, as if he or she had pneumonia; and, just as for pneumonia, a diagnosis can be made and appropriate treatment instituted only by a qualified professional. Attempting to classify or dismiss the disorder ourselves — as the "blues" or a "phase" — can be dangerous.

How dangerous? Latest figures indicate there are 30,000 confirmed suicides a year in the United States; a great many more are misclassified as "accidents." Suicide is the second leading cause of death among young adults. The suicide rate among fifteen- to twenty-four-year-old people has risen 150 percent in twenty years. Simply stated, a clinically significant depression is a potentially fatal illness. People can die from it.

Parents need to be aware that two of the profound psychiatric disorders that first surface in young adulthood — clinical depression (which includes manic-depressive illness) and schizophrenia — are now seen by mental health professionals as having a biological base. Unfortunately, our attitudes toward these disorders have not kept pace with the scientific advances in understanding them. Often we continue to view the young adult in trouble as somehow lacking in morals or deficient in character, or think we've done something wrong in raising him or her. All too frequently, early warning signs of schizophrenia and clinical depression are viewed as "the kid's being wild and crazy" or "she's just lazy and unmotivated." In order to handle their child's behavior, many parents want and need to believe "it's just a phase."

"You're just feeling sorry for yourself" was what Paul, a Seattleite, told his twenty-three-year-old daughter, Greta, after she had been living at home for a few weeks. Greta's two-year involvement with her boyfriend had ended with his decision to move to New York. At the same time, her roommate, a young woman she had known since high school, announced she was getting married and moving out of the apartment they shared.

Terribly upset, Greta had moved back home with her parents. Paul and Marjorie, both in their fifties, had agreed that she could stay until she found a new roommate or a workable shared housing situation. Greta was the oldest of their three children; her two younger brothers were away at college and doing well. Like so many parents of boomerang kids, Paul and Marjorie had thought they were finally free.

Greta managed to get to work every day at her secretarial job in a public relations firm, but in the evenings she was tearful and withdrawn. She had difficulty sleeping, had no appetite, and began losing weight. Her parents' efforts to cheer her up were met with irritability and apathy. As the weeks went by, her father kept pointing out all the things she had going for her and telling her to think about all the other people in the world who had bigger problems. He began to chide her, telling her to "stop feeling sorry for yourself," but her depression deepened. After a month, both parents began to encourage her to move out, telling her she needed to be with people her own age and to make a fresh start. Each night when she returned home from work they asked her if she had done anything about finding a place of her own. Greta felt pressured and had increasing difficulty concentrating at work. She began to fear she would lose her job. Feeling hopeless and unable to cope, she confessed to her mother, "Sometimes I just don't feel like living." Her mother told her that she had everything to live for and to put those silly thoughts out of her head. She told Greta, "I won't stand for hearing any talk like that." Greta felt trapped and alone. Several nights after her conversation with her mother, she got drunk and impulsively cut her wrists while her parents were out for the evening. When they found her, her parents rushed Greta to the emergency room of a nearby hospital. She was treated medically and then admitted to the psychiatric unit. Only then did her parents realize the seriousness of the situation.

Greta's initial unhappiness seemed more or less natural: she'd lost two important people in her life and, when she came home, was grieving for them as well as her lost independence. However, her unhappiness did not, as would be natural, abate with time. As in Greta's case, most of the signs of a clinical depression are indistinguishable from normal mourning in the beginning; it's their persistence and deepening over some weeks that is often the first clue that a "mourning reaction" is sliding into a medically significant depression requiring treatment. Like many physical illnesses, depression can clear with time, but it often takes four or five months. With appropriate treatment, its symptoms can be managed, the risk it poses to life reduced, and the resulting injury minimized.

## Signs of Depression

Mental health professionals have adopted, after long study, a series of diagnostic criteria to determine whether someone is sufficiently depressed to warrant psychological treatment: psychotherapy with or without antidepressant medications. In simple terms, here's roughly what they look for:

1. Any change in sleeping? The classic sign is waking early in the morning and being unable to get back to sleep (waking at four o'clock when one used to sleep until seven o'clock, for example); often taking longer than a half hour to fall asleep is a sign, too. Sleeping less than usual (five hours when it used to be eight, for example) or more than usual (staying in bed until noon) are also biological signs of a depression.

2. How about appetite and weight? A loss of appetite,

and then weight, can be a sign of depression; so can a significant increase in both.

3. How about overall activity? A noticeable restlessness, or agitation, can be a sign of depression; so can a significant slowing down. There are both "agitated" and "retarded" depressions.

4. Has there been a loss of interest in things? Does there seem to be a sense that nothing pleasurable exists anymore? A loss of interest in sex, or in anything significant, for that matter, can be an important symptom.

5. Has the usual energy level changed? If the person feels sluggish, is extremely and easily fatigued, or seems overwhelmed by relatively minor tasks, this is worth noting.

6. Are there indications that he or she feels worthless or blames him- or herself excessively or inappropriately?

7. Do you see evidence of difficulty concentrating or thinking, or an inability to stay focused on something, such as reading or watching a televison show? Slower thinking and unusual difficulty making decisions can be symptoms as well.

8. Are there references to death, or comments about suicide, or statements about not wanting to go on with life and wishing it were over? *Any* evidence of a subtle suicide attempt, even something as indirect as drunken driving, for example? Has he or she given away possessions to friends or family members?

A medically significant depression is not to be confused with a normal sadness that young adults may feel transiently as they separate from their families. As mentioned in chapter two, many young adults going through the process of emotionally separating from their parents may naturally feel somewhat depressed and be unusually vulnerable. Other losses at this particular time can be felt more acutely, however, and may send them spiraling into a clinical depression that goes well beyond this temporary grieving. Professional help is needed when at least four of the criteria above are present and have persisted without interruption for over two weeks. Suggesting a professional consultation for the young adult who exhibits such behavior is not overreacting; such help may save his or her life. How much better to have gotten advice that may not have been needed than to live with the guilt and grief of not having acted in time!

Greta's parents loved her and tried to be helpful, but their well-intentioned efforts to cheer her up only added to her feelings of worthlessness and inadequacy. When they reminded her that other people were worse off, she felt they were saying she had no right to her feelings, and that she was unacceptable for feeling the way she did. Statements like these, well-meaning as they were, actually contributed to her deepening depression.

## What Your Depressed Son or Daughter Needs from You

What does a depressed son or daughter need? Here are some suggestions:

1. Keep in mind that depression changes how people feel about themselves, especially their sense of self-worth. While a depressed individual's bleak outlook may seem totally unrealistic to us, it feels real to him or her. Don't contradict someone who is depressed, no matter how distorted what he or she is saying seems to you at the time; this contradiction simply emphasizes your differences at the very time that person most needs to feel a sense of connection. You don't have to agree, but you do need to accept this as his or her view of things. There's nothing wrong with saying that your viewpoint

is different, and you can even go so far as to suggest that the young adult may see things differently at another time. Accepting a son or daughter's seemingly skewed view of self and his or her place in the world can be enormously difficult when it doesn't make sense to you; but when you deny a young adult's expressions of worthlessness and hopelessness, his or her irritability, which is often part of the depression, widens the gulf between you even further. "I know this is a hard time for you" will work a lot better than "Cheer up, it's not so bad"; a person who is depressed can't see anything to cheer up about, and it *is* bad — to the individual. Generally positive statements can be helpful, even if they don't seem to get through, *but only if accompanied by some recognition of the depressed individual's viewpoint.* For example, a statement like "I know you feel lousy right now, but I still know how much talent and brains you have" can be comforting, whereas saying, "You have so much talent and brains, I wish you could recognize it" implies that the depressed person is inadequate for not recognizing his or her value. The key part of the first statement is the phrase "I know you feel lousy right now."

2. Encourage activity. Exercise can reduce depressive symptoms, and it may even influence the altered brain chemistry of a depression. Walking is a good choice for someone who's apathetic, and is also a useful outlet for someone who's agitated; offering to go along yourself might make it easier. Although he or she is suffering, and at times intensely so, a depressed person isn't an invalid who needs to spend the day in bed with the curtains drawn. Ask and expect the person to help with housework, particularly routine tasks you can do together, such as washing dishes or laundry, and let him or her know you appreciate the contribution. Psychi-

atric hospitals often use this approach through their "therapeutic community" where patients make their own beds, clean up the ward, help with meals and snacks, and organize some of their own activities.

3. Keep your expectations realistic, though, and in line with a depressed person's temporarily reduced ability to function. The "instant solution" and emphasis on achievement that's typical of today's life-style puts even more pressure on the depressed person struggling with daily fatigue and inertia. Of course you want your son or daughter to get better, to "snap out of it," but a clinical depression can take months to run its course. Dropping the expectation that he or she — or you, for that matter — can change things quickly will relieve some of the pressure that contributes to the depression.

4. It may help to present yourself as human and fallible, to let your son or daughter know that you've had some rough times and felt pretty awful sometimes (although unless you've had a clinical depression yourself and can remember what it was like, don't pretend your experiences were the same). A depressed person can be terribly self-critical, and can feel bad just for being depressed. If you can be less judgmental about yourself, it may help your son or daughter to feel less different and alienated.

## Getting Professional Help

Dealing with a clinically depressed person is not easy. You're not a therapist, you're a parent. Your life has already been interrupted by the return home of the young adult, and you have your own feelings to manage, too. One of the best things you can do for both of you is to encourage, in as nonthreatening, nonjudgmental a way as you can, the young adult to get some professional help. It shouldn't sound as though you're ashamed or see the young person as a failure. Therapy (with or without medication) is more acceptable than it once was, but the stigma attached to mental or emotional problems still persists. American values such as self-reliance and individual effort are deeply ingrained in all of us, but there are times when it's necessary and important to find the courage to ask for help.

Most of us are generally comfortable with seeing a doctor for a broken bone, but not a broken mind. We tend to see emotional problems as somehow different from physical ones, overlooking or perhaps never understanding that the body and mind are part of the same system. Physical factors such as hormonal disorders or the side effects of certain medications can lead to depression, and psychological depression often results in measurable changes in the body's biochemical makeup. Several medications specifically relieve depressive symptoms, confirming that one's body chemistry and mood are often closely linked. Frederick Goodwin, the scientific director of the National Institute of Mental Health, said, "Depression is the richest, most striking example in psychiatry — maybe in all of medicine — of the relationship between biological vulnerability and the psychological stresses of life."[1]

You might approach your adult child about seeing a mental health professional in this way: "You know that if you had a bad stomachache that didn't go away, we'd want you to see a doctor. We wouldn't expect you to cure yourself. We think you might be depressed, and it's been hanging on a while, and there may be something chemically out of balance. We really want you to have things checked out. Besides, an outsider — someone more objective than we can be, as parents — might help, especially someone trained to sort out things about depression."

## Manic-Depressive Disorder

Another related psychiatric disorder that usually has its
first onset in young adulthood is manic-depressive illness.
It falls in the same category as clinical depression, but
differs in that the depressive episodes alternate with what
are called manic episodes, or periods of hyperactivity.

When Jamie, twenty, dropped out of college and returned home his parents thought at first that the changes
they saw in him were just part of his efforts to "find himself."
He told them that he really wasn't sure why he was in
college and was unsure of the major he had to declare by
the beginning of the next semester. He wanted to take some
time out to work for a while and figure things out. His
parents agreed that it might not make sense for him to
continue college until he knew what he wanted.

Jamie had always been a gregarious and talkative young
man. When he first returned home, his parents noticed that
he seemed extra talkative and excitable, but they thought
perhaps he was just anxious about having left college. The
first few days he was home he wasn't able to sleep more
than a few hours a night; as the week wore on he didn't
sleep at all. He said he really didn't need sleep, that he felt
great. He had boundless energy and talked about poetry
he had been up writing all night, and grand schemes of
how the poetry was going to make a profound contribution
to the understanding of the universe. At the end of the
week, Jamie began to be convinced that he was "chosen"
at this time in his life to experience and convey to everyone
in the world the true meaning of life. He talked rapidly as
one thought sped into another. One morning at breakfast
his speech seemed to take off in an uncontrolled flight of
ideas: "Breakfast, you know, break the fast, like the Last
Supper, only He was betrayed, only He didn't know it, the
wine was going to be His blood, like this tomato juice, so

innocent and yet I may be betrayed, but there's vitamin C in tomatoes, see the C, ha-ha-ha, but who can really see, only Darth Vader knows. . . ." He talked on and on incessantly and seemed compelled to keep moving. He was incapable of sitting quietly and was unable to watch television with his parents without incessantly talking and interpreting every scene in the program as some profound message that fit with his new view of the universe. His parents were confused. Their suggestions that he "try to be realistic" were met with irritability and sometimes hostility. Jamie was impulsive and out of control. He said he was a "special" person destined for greatness and the rules of society didn't apply to him. His parent began to suspect he was high on drugs. When they confronted him, he flew into a rage and fled in the family car. When he didn't return that evening, his parents called the police and described the situation. Jamie was picked up and taken to the hospital psychiatric unit, where he was diagnosed as having a manic episode. What his parents did not know was that prior to his return home he had become quite depressed, exhibiting all the symptoms of the clinical depression we discussed early in this chapter. When he returned home, he became agitated and the depression shifted to mania.

## Signs of Manic-Depressive Illness

Psychiatrists now refer to manic-depressive illness as a bipolar disorder, which simply means that the depression and the mania are opposite ends of the same illness. Besides checking for signs of depression, psychiatrists also look for signs of a manic (excited) episode lasting a week or more, in which there is an expansive or irritable mood with at least three or four of the behaviors listed below:

1. Is the young person unusually active or restless socially, sexually, or on the job?

2. Is he or she unusually talkative, or seeming compelled to talk, unable to remain quiet?
3. Do his or her ideas seem to jump from one place to another, making them hard to follow in conversation, or has there been a mention of thoughts that seem to be "racing," "speeding," "hard to keep up with"?
4. Is the young person unusually self-important, or downright grandiose, in viewing him- or herself?
5. Does he or she seem to need remarkably little sleep (perhaps as little as two or three hours daily)?
6. Is he or she easily distracted, shifting concentration from one thing to another rapidly, unable to stay at one task?
7. Is he or she excessively involved in activities that sound as though uncharacteristically poor judgment is being exercised (buying sprees, sudden trips without much reason, highly questionable business investments, large loans, impulsively starting or ending relationships)?

Sometimes an episode doesn't go far enough to be called manic, but it can qualify as hypomanic, which means it is less severe. A genuinely manic episode involves enough change in mood, thinking, and activity that it's pretty obvious that something is wrong, but the milder episodes of hypomania are more subtle. These may be missed by the family, and can require professional expertise to detect.

The most important thing to remember about these "affective" or emotional disorders — depression and bipolar illness — is that they respond well to psychotherapy and medication. Scientists at the National Institute of Mental Health estimate that, with appropriate treatment, between 80 and 90 percent of people suffering from depression and bipolar illness can be helped substantially, and that with professional help many of the remaining ones can improve.[2]

## Schizophrenia

The picture for schizophrenia is also somewhat brighter than it once was. Young adulthood, between eighteen and twenty-four years of age, is the most susceptible period for the onset of schizophrenia. Although schizophrenia is the classic disease of madness, we think Dr. Silvano Arieti's definition is the most helpful. He calls schizophrenia "an abnormal condition of the mind that affects only human beings; drastically changes their modes of thinking, feeling, and dealing with the world; *makes them confuse fantasy with reality;* and leads them to maladaptive ways of living."[3]

The diagnosis of schizophrenia includes a serious loss of contact with reality (the definition of a psychosis) and significantly altered patterns of thinking. This is why it's called a "thought disorder" rather than an "affective" one, although in fact one's whole personality is disturbed by it. Schizophrenics will often hold on to bizarre beliefs that could have no basis in reality — beliefs that their thoughts are being broadcast to others, or that others are inserting thoughts into their mind, or that they are being spied on by the television set. These absurd beliefs are called delusions and can be grandiose, religious, or jealous in nature. Schizophrenics often hallucinate as well, having experiences rather like waking dreams in which most often they hear voices or unusual sounds, although sight or smell can also be part of the hallucinations. Their speech can become incoherent. Most of all, schizophrenics exhibit signs of marked deterioration in their level of organization and functioning at work, in social relations, and ordinary self-care, and an unusual social isolation and withdrawal from others that is more profound than in depression.

Schizophrenia seems primarily a biological disorder with a strong genetic component; it clearly runs in families. If you have an identical twin who develops schizophrenia, you have a high probability (perhaps 80 percent) of developing it yourself. The more distant the biological relative with the disorder, the less your chance of developing it. A young person can develop this serious disorder, however, with no family history of it. It can appear anytime in life, although young adulthood is the most probable time for it to start. While it is not due to stress, its onset is often stress-related and therefore worth mentioning because of the considerable stress many of the young adults who return home experience.

Young adults who can't adapt to the physical separation from home, and whose return is accompanied by widespread and marked changes in personality, may be showing the first warning signs of schizophrenia. Generally, they will be more withdrawn, shutting themselves up in their rooms for hours, although a smaller number will show signs of unusually outgoing or flippant behavior. They may be agitated, intrusive, and quite sensitive; often a series of family "misunderstandings" will arise, which become more and more serious. The victims can seem anxious, insecure, and erratic, seeking reassurance one moment and the next suddenly attacking family members as being "too critical." They may accuse various family members or the group as a whole of trying to harm them. Because these young people _have_ started to crumble inside, they begin to feel inadequate and incompetent, lacking in confidence; it is at this time that the grandiose delusions of their own importance appear in a desperate attempt to restore self-esteem.

It's not always easy to differentiate between normal personality shifts in a young adult searching for identity, and the warning signs of a serious illness such as schizophrenia. Young adults slow to mature may normally still exhibit periods of uncertainty, rebelliousness, and unusual patterns of behavior characteristic of adolescence. But these stormy periods in the healthy young adult are short-lived and lead to personality growth and more mature functioning. In schizophrenics these patterns persist and worsen, and lead to impaired functioning and a potentially limited life.

The exact causes of schizophrenia remain a mystery; however, today most scientists are focusing on biological causes. Recent laboratory studies indicate that the brain structure and chemistry of schizophrenics differ from those of normal individuals, and modern investigators have concluded that a mixture of environmental and biological factors must come together to result in this tragic illness. The question about which is more important is a matter for continuing scientific scrutiny, but it seems clear now that solely blaming family influences for this disease created unnecessary pain for the families of schizophrenics, adding guilt to the agony of watching a loved one turn into a disturbed stranger.[4]

The prognosis for schizophrenics is much more encouraging than it once was. Two-thirds improve enough to live satisfactory lives; many recover completely. Psychiatrists have seen former patients go on to achieve success in the business world, in the arts, in academic life, and in other spheres.[5]

If you observe a personality change or bizarre behavior in your adult child, seek help. Perhaps it is "just a phase," but it's better to err on the side of caution. If, in fact, he or she *is* suffering from a psychiatric disorder, chances are good that it may be in part the result of a chemical imbalance within the brain, and that it may respond to treatment with medication.

## Drug and Alcohol Addiction

Young adults in unprecedented numbers are becoming addicted to drugs and alcohol, most often using a combination of cocaine, marijuana, and liquor. According to the National Institute on Drug Abuse, the ranks of cocaine users alone increased from 15 million to 22 million between 1979 and 1982, with the largest segment of this abuser population young adults. The *Harvard Medical School Mental Health Letter* has reported that high doses or repeated use of cocaine can produce a state resembling mania, with impaired judgment, incessant rambling talk, hyperactivity, and paranoia that may lead to violence or accidents. Serious acute physical reactions to the drug are also possible. People who have high blood pressure or damaged arteries may suffer strokes. Convulsions may lead to fatal cardiac arrest. In fact, the reported number of deaths involving cocaine has risen from fewer than a dozen to more than two hundred a year over the last decade.[6] And, this report was written in 1985, *before* the arrival of a type of cocaine known as "crack," a form that multiplies the dangers of coke *five to ten times!*

Parents usually find it impossible to cope with the antisocial behavior that often accompanies the addiction of their adult children; lying, stealing, verbal and physical abusiveness, and other violent behavior leave parents feeling enraged, helpless, and impotent. You don't have to cope with it! Your adult child should not be allowed to return home if he or she is unwilling to get treatment. Young adults need to face the often terrifying consequences of a decision not to get help. *If you have adult children addicted to drugs or alcohol, you only support them in their addiction if you allow them to live at home without being enrolled in a drug treatment program.* Love is not enough, and the love you express in allowing them to return home must be conditional on their getting professional help. If they refuse to get help or if repeated efforts fail and their antisocial behavior persists, then, difficult as it is, you must accept the fact that you cannot allow your adult child to return home — and forgive yourself for the decision.

This is where many parents get stuck. The idea of not taking a child in, especially one who is down and out and in serious trouble, flies in the face of all we have been taught to be as parents. Somewhere all of us as parents got the idea that we must love and accept our children unconditionally, no matter what. This is valid when our children are infants. A parent can and should love and accept and take care of an infant no matter how much the baby cries and wakes you up in the middle of the night or demands your attention. But we do *not* have to tolerate lying, stealing, or verbally and physically abusive and violent behavior from an adult child. Your job as a parent now is to demand that he or she get professional help, steering him or her to that help. Nothing is negotiable here. If he or she refuses, then you must shut the door to your home, no longer willing to tolerate such turmoil and abuse.

It helps to remember it's the door to your *home* you're shutting, but not to your heart; in fact, saying this final "No" can be the most loving thing you do. Some doors must be closed if they are ever to be truly open again. Sometimes the only hope for those who are violent and out of control is to experience the loss of family and be forced to face themselves. Some people can't get help until they hit bottom.

Exactly when do you throw your adult child out? When you feel you have done everything you possibly could to convince him or her to get help and/or when you have reached your limit. This differs from family to family. One family reached its limit when a twenty-three-year-old son who refused to recognize that his drinking was a problem hit his mother when he was drunk; another family reached its limit only after the daughter, a cocaine addict, repeatedly stole from her parents, wrecked the family car, and ran up exorbitant bills on her father's credit cards. Each time she was confronted, she promised never to let it happen again. When she stole her mother's jewelry, something snapped and the family was able to say, "No more. You cannot live here anymore. We will have a relationship with you only if you are in a drug program and are drug-free."

You are apt to feel terribly guilty about taking such a stand, not only because you are used to thinking you are supposed to love your child unconditionally, but because at some level you worry that you may be the reason your adult child is having such serious problems. Your guilt reflects all the times in your child's early life when you feel you were neglectful and made mistakes. You undoubtedly *did* make some mistakes. All parents do, in varying degrees. The point is, that was then and this is now, and past mistakes don't entitle adult children to demand that their parents eternally make restitution by taking abuse from them. The most you can do today is get help for a disturbed adult child, forgive yourself for the past, and know that, in the interest of the ongoing safety and health of your family, the violent and disruptive young adult must not be allowed to live at home.

The serious problems we have discussed in this chapter are disorders for which professional help is essential. However, emotionally separating from the family is stressful for all young adults, and the benefits of psychotherapy are not limited to those with acute problems. Many young adults, as they struggle to separate and carve out their own unique identity, can turn their lives around with therapy. If you feel your son or daughter is not seriously disturbed but could benefit from therapy nonetheless, don't hesitate to suggest it.

# SEVEN

---

# Lemonade From Lemons

## *The Benefits of the Return Home*

---

LEMONADE FROM LEMONS, clouds with silver linings, the proverbial second chance — there really are benefits for both the parents and the young adult when a son or daughter boomerangs back home, even though most parents understandably find it pretty hard to see much that's positive about the crisis that triggers the return. At first it *is* difficult to find much good in the fact that a young adult has gone through a divorce, flunked out of school, or experienced a loss or a failure of one kind or another, coming home hurting, depressed, and wounded.

In the Chinese language the word *crisis* is formed by two separate characters; one means "danger" and the other "opportunity." It's an apt juxtaposition. Often people grow through their pain and attain new heights; the human spirit must transcend its former limits in order to survive a crisis and move on.

Many parents felt they had an opportunity to parent in a better, healthier way when their adult child returned home; they felt they had been given a second chance at being a more successful parent. It became an opportunity that allowed them to relate to their young adult in a growth-producing, life-enhancing way. "I'm a very different person now than I was when my son was little," "I just couldn't help her when she was an adolescent — I had too many problems of my own," and "Thank God I can be there for him now, as the person I am today" are typical of the responses we heard from many parents. Having themselves matured, they now had more to give than when they were younger, and they experienced the return home of their adult child as a chance to love in a new way.

Psychotherapy is sometimes called a "corrective emotional experience," but corrective emotional experiences certainly aren't the exclusive domain of therapists and clients. Parents and their adult children can learn to develop new interactions that can go a long way toward repairing and healing formerly troubled relationships and injuries from the past. For some of the families we talked with, the return of their adult child was an opportunity to develop a gratifying relationship for the first time. It was like that for Darla, a forty-six-year-old single parent, and her twenty-three-year-old daughter, Maggie.

When we first met Darla and Maggie, we noticed the easy, companionable way they related to each other. We talked with them on a rainy Saturday afternoon in the living room of Darla's condominium. It was a pleasant, comforting room warmly decorated in earth tones; bookshelves and tables overflowed with books, and plants of all sizes and descriptions were thriving everywhere. There was a pot of tea and a plate of cookies on the coffee table.

Darla motioned to the teapot: "It's herbal tea — Maggie's got me hooked on the stuff, but I can fix you a cup of coffee if you'd like."

"You can't pass up Mom's cookies," Maggie chimed in. "She's finally become domestic — I call her Mrs. Fields for encouragement."

It was clear that they were good friends. When we commented on it, they both laughed and were quick to point out that this hadn't always been true.

"When I was in high school, Mom and I fought all the time. Sometimes we'd go for days without speaking to each other, and then something would set one of us off and we'd start screaming all over again." Maggie ran her hand through her closely cropped blond hair, and then looked out the window. "I don't really like to think about those times."

"It's not my favorite chapter in our lives, either." Darla took a sip of her tea and put the cup down. "I might as well tell you — I had a serious drinking problem when Maggie was in high school. For a few years, I was an alcoholic. Maggie's father divorced me when Maggie was a junior and I didn't handle it very well, to say the least."

Darla went on to explain that she and Maggie's father had been married when they were quite young, right after high school, and that she had never gone to college or worked outside the home. "My family was my whole life. I wasn't too different from a lot of women in my generation raised in the fifties. The divorce totally devastated me. I tried to numb everything with drinking; I thought being in a stupor was better than being in such despair — so terribly depressed. I hated the depression. It was as though I was stuck in this awful blackness, a kind of crippling dread — and it wasn't the first time in my life I had been like that. Maggie's father was in the army when we were first married — he was in Vietnam from 1966 to 1968 and I remember very little of those years, when Maggie was three to five. Actually, about all I remember is plunking her down in front of the TV to watch 'Sesame Street' while I slept. I felt like I spent those two years curled up in a ball. I didn't understand that I was ill — that I had a serious depression. I just thought I was lazy and somehow intrinsically inadequate as a person. I blamed myself, and that just made it all worse. I know Maggie and her older brother,

Nick, were hurt by it — those early years are so important, although Nick was older and in school, and I don't think he was affected quite as much."

Maggie added, "What was so hard when they got divorced was watching what happened to Mom. It wasn't that hard for me to have Dad leave. I hardly remember him being around; it wasn't just when I was little that he was gone. He was always working late or away on business."

"I think he stayed in the marriage out of duty. We hadn't been happy together for years," Darla went on. "I stayed because divorce was unthinkable and I had no idea how I'd make it otherwise. We were both Catholic. Divorce wasn't an easy alternative for him either, but I think he was kind of biding his time until the kids were old enough so he felt he could leave. He filed for divorce not long after Maggie turned sixteen. I was terrified."

Darla told us that the divorce agreement specified that her ex-husband would pay for a college education for her, as well as monthly maintenance payments until she had her degree. "Even though I was enrolled in college, I'd come back after class and get drunk every night. Maggie and I had terrible fights every time I'd tell her what time to come home or tried to offer any kind of suggestion about her behavior. Whenever I'd try and act like a mother, she'd confront me with my behavior; we'd scream at each other and then she'd ignore me."

Maggie shook her head. "I really ran wild those years — I don't know how I managed to graduate from high school."

"Or I from college, I had such a bad start at it." Darla took a deep breath, then she smiled. "You know, the other night I heard a woman being interviewed on a radio talk show and she was talking about guilt. She said that people of different religions have different ways of feeling guilt — Protestant guilt is because what you did has offended God,

Jewish guilt is because what you just did has ripped the heart out of your mother, and Catholic guilt is when the entire balance of the universe hangs on what you just did. I thought the definitions were just great — and as a Catholic I've sure had to work to push that kind of guilt out of the way — for failing Maggie, not just at the time of divorce, but for when she was little."

"But we did it, Mom."

"Did what?"

"We both graduated — me from high school and you from college and guilt."

As they looked at each other and smiled, we could sense the strength of the love between them. Maggie then told us that after she graduated from high school and went away to college in Oregon, her mother went to Alcoholics Anonymous and had been sober ever since. It was clear she was proud of her.

Why did Maggie boomerang home? We learned that she had never finished college, dropping out at the end of her freshman year. While her mother was getting her education and attending AA meetings, Maggie had fallen in love with a senior who had been accepted at law school. They decided to live together, finding an inexpensive place in student housing. Maggie worked as a receptionist in a dental office to support them until he finished law school. The plan was that it would be her turn to finish her education after he graduated and was practicing law. It never happened. Not long after he joined a Portland law firm he wanted out of the relationship, and Maggie came back to Seattle to move in with Darla.

"The ironic thing," Maggie said with a half-smile, "was how much what I had done mirrored the life Mom had when she first married Dad. Sure, I never got married and that probably gave me the mistaken idea that I was different — but I really wasn't that different. I built my whole life around this man and when it didn't work, I felt like I had nothing of my own. I was a mess."

"It was terribly hard to see Maggie hurt like that when she first came home, because I knew exactly how she felt. Perhaps this sounds silly, but it seemed like God had given me another chance to be there for her. I had been sober for four years, and I was stronger than I had ever been in my life." Darla's voice broke. "I could be her mom."

Maggie wanted to make sure that we didn't think she was being babied by her mother and treated like a little kid. "I'm going to college and I have a part-time job. I pay Mom rent, and we've divided up all the housework; it's like we're two adult roommates. The thing that's so special, though, is that she is my mom and for the first time I can talk to her when I need to — about all kinds of things, and that really helps. She's kind of a role model for me, too. This independent woman she's become."

"Sometimes I feel like we're really learning things together, but it does feel great to know that I can emotionally be there for Maggie, now. And we have a lot of fun together, too. I feel blessed."

When Maggie returned home, she and her mother had the chance to repair a relationship that had been a very troubled one. Darla had changed; she now had the capacity to nurture and support her daughter. Even though Darla was aware of how guilty she felt, she didn't infantilize Maggie or accept her daughter back unconditionally; instead she expected her to share costs and responsibility. The healing, comfort, and nurturing she gave Maggie encouraged her to grow.

## Saying "No"

Tim and Jessie, both in their fifties, are a Boulder couple who also saw the return home of their boomerang kid as a chance to relate in a new and better way. When we talked with them, their twenty-six-year-old son, Neil, had been living with them for ten months.

Tim was a trial lawyer, and a talkative, outgoing person. "You know, a lot of our friends are having trouble with their grown kids," he said, "and we hear a lot of them blaming themselves. The main thing I hear at the office from one of my partners is how hard he worked and how he regrets that his career took so much time from the family. Well, I'll tell you, and you can write this down, it's just the opposite with us. We did too much for our kids."

"Especially Neil," Jessie added. "He was our only boy, and the youngest. He was a bright, creative kid and we were totally involved in his life."

"We thought he hung the moon — and we acted like that, too. I know now we didn't do him any favors."

As Tim and Jessie explained how they had related to Neil when he was growing up, it became obvious that they fit the pattern of the childcentric family discussed in chapter two.

Jessie was a traditional housewife; although she had some volunteer activities outside the home, her world revolved around her children. She spent hours helping Neil with homework and school projects, chauffeuring him to music and art lessons, and watching his weekend sports activities. For many years, his father had coached a soccer team that Neil played on. Tim and Jessie had expected very little family responsibility of their son. Jessie cooked all his meals, cleaned his room, and did his laundry; about all that was required of Neil was that he be his bright, creative, high-achieving self. Throughout his childhood and adolescence, Neil's parents celebrated even his most minor triumphs. They had relished his every achievement and cheered each accomplishment; when Neil left for college at age eighteen, he quite naturally expected that the world, too, would treat him in the same special way.

Neil quickly found out that he was *not* the center of the universe for his roommate, his professors, or anyone else. The professors didn't seem to care one way or another if he came to class (if they even noticed him at all among the other 175 in his freshman classes), and his roommate didn't beam at and cheer for his every accomplishment. After a difficult first year, Neil announced to his parents that he was dropping out, that his one true goal was to make it big in the art world. He rented a room in a large old house that he shared with four other young adults, found a part-time job as a dishwasher, and asked his parents to buy him hundreds of dollars' worth of art supplies and contribute to his living expenses while he tried to make it as a painter. They agreed.

"We thought it was just a phase that he was going through. Neil had been so unmotivated and confused at college, we didn't see any point in putting pressure on him," his father said. "My life at his age had been nothing but work. My family was not well-off; I put myself through college and law school working two jobs and taking out loans. I thought if Neil wanted to take some time to find himself we could afford to help him out and it might be a good thing."

"I agreed with Tim," Jessie said. "Things had not been easy for my family financially, either, and I suppose we were the typical parents that wanted things to be better for our kids."

The "phase" Tim thought Neil was going through lasted seven years. It was seven years of moving from job to job (all part-time unskilled labor) and moving from house to house, periodically moving back home with Mom and Dad. Neil did have some talent as a painter and managed to sell a few paintings, each time believing he would soon have his big break and no longer need the perpetual cash handouts from his parents. But the big break never came. Each time Neil boomeranged home to live, his childhood pattern of irresponsibility continued, as Jessie picked up right where she had left off, cleaning his room, doing his laundry, and cooking his meals. And each time he asked for money, his father opened his wallet.

"I was the quintessential soft touch," Tim said, "but it all changed about a year ago. I'm not exactly sure how it all quite relates, but a little over a year ago my father died of cancer. We had never been close, I doubt he ever thought about being close to his kids, but he tried to teach us about the value of a dollar and an honest day's work. He was a rigid guy, quite gruff and strict and a tough disciplinarian. To tell you the truth, I was afraid of him when I was a kid. We never talked much, but I respected him. He was a hard worker, and he met his obligations. He worked all his life in the post office. He was not a success by some standards; he never made a lot of money. But he had my respect, and my sister's and brother's as well. I'm not sure there's much that's more important than that. When my father died I thought about myself as a father, and I thought about my son; I knew that I didn't respect my son, and worst of all — and this hit me over the head like a ton of bricks — it was my fault."

"Ours," Jessie said quietly.

"Well, okay — it was our fault. Well, after my father's funeral, I told Jessie that the next time Neil asked to come home — and I knew there'd be a next time, as sure as I knew the sun would rise in the east — we were going to say 'yes,' but only if he would agree to certain conditions. And this was the hardest part — if he didn't agree to our conditions, then our answer was unequivocally 'no.' "

"I can't tell you how hard it was for Tim and me to come to that," Jessie said. "It was easier to keep buying into the idea that this was only temporary, only a phase.

But Tim was adamant and that helped me — I know this must sound foolish, but I think I always felt deep down that if I said 'no' to my kids they might not love me, so I just kept doing everything for them."

Jessie and Tim worked together on the list of conditions under which they would allow Neil to live at home again. "Every time we got bogged down," Jessie said, "we'd try and pretend it was a business arrangement we were making with a stranger, as if we were becoming a rooming house. It made it easier. When I'd say something like how it wasn't that much work for me to do Neil's laundry, Tim would ask if I'd do the laundry for a boarder. Of course I wouldn't, and looking at it that way helped."

"We knew we had to get our expectations clear between us so we could present a nonnegotiable, united front. And we knew each other's weaknesses."

"Mine was falling into doing all the mothering stuff for him," Jessie admitted.

"And mine was not being able to refuse him money," Tim explained; "so we made a pact that if we felt ourselves weakening we had to go to the other for support. After all, we were trying to change a twenty-seven-year habit, and we knew it wasn't going to be easy."

"The specifics we came up with," Jessie added, "were pretty straightforward, although it took the two of us days to figure it all out. Neil was to be treated exactly like a boarder. He would pay rent, a sum the three of us would agree on; he would do his own laundry, and pay for any long distance calls; he would be expected to clean the common territory — living room, kitchen, bathroom — on a rotating basis. When we first started the arrangement we considered that the sum Neil paid included room and board, and we ran into a lot of problems. Sometimes Neil would be home for dinner and sometimes he wouldn't — it was hard for me to plan, and we were wasting a lot of food.

Neil didn't like feeling that he was committed to be here, and he was the one who suggested that we really ought to operate in every way like a true shared housing situation where he'd buy his own food and have his own shelf in the refrigerator. It seemed pretty cold at first for him not to be able to eat our food, but we agreed that we did want to be businesslike and not continue to provide an atmosphere where he could be indulged like a small child. So we gave it a try."

"And it was true, the hardest part for Jessie was Neil having his own shelf in the refrigerator and not sharing our food."

"True! It was agony," Jessie laughed, "and collecting the rent was awful for Tim."

"Every time he'd hand me this check that he'd worked for all week at five dollars an hour, I'd have to keep telling myself that I was doing him a favor by making him pay me. I did a lot of talking to myself, believe me. The first few months were the hardest. But I know what we're doing for him is right, and I feel like Jessie and I are helping him in a way we never did before. Best of all — it's working. I just feel lucky that we've had a chance to set it right before it was too late."

"It was hard to admit I was worried that my kids wouldn't love me if I said 'no' to them, but the irony is that the way things are now, Neil has been more loving than ever before. I feel close to him and really enjoy him."

Neil has lived at home under these conditions for the past ten months. He is saving money for first and last month's rent and a damage deposit on an apartment. He thinks he should have enough saved to move out in another four months. After we talked with Tim and Jessie, we talked with Neil to get his viewpoint on living with his parents under the new regime.

"Well, it was a shock at first when all these new conditions were laid out, because I thought I was going to move back just like all those other times, no questions asked. And frankly, I didn't quite believe that they meant it at first, it was such an about-face. But when I asked Dad for loans a couple of times and he said 'no,' I found out pretty quick they weren't kidding."

Neil didn't seem bitter or frustrated when he talked about the new demands. When we commented on how accepting he seemed of the situation, he said, "You know, for the first time, I don't feel like a little kid when I talk to my parents — it's a lot like we're friends. It's strange, but paying my own way has brought me a new kind of freedom — I feel like I can do or say whatever I want. It's not that I didn't do what I wanted before, but I always felt so guilty and obligated because they were always there bailing me out. And I've gotten much more serious about painting. I've realized that if I'm committed to a career in fine arts it's going to be financially difficult, and I'll probably always have to work at some other job to support my art. I know now that the world is not going to go crazy over my art the way my parents used to get so excited about every single clay or crayon thing I'd make at school. I actually feel like my parents are taking me seriously for the first time by having these expectations, and it's enabled me to take myself seriously. If I'm going to make it as an artist, I'm the only one that can make it happen."

Neil told us how much he was looking forward to having his own apartment. "You'd be surprised how many people there are my age that are used to people doing everything for them, and don't know anything about give and take. It's an attitude I'm trying to change; I've gotten real tired of it in myself and other people. I'm kind of like the re-formed smoker that goes nuts around anyone who smokes. I remember this one time in a house I shared with four other guys. The dishes piled up for a week, and everyone in the house said they weren't his dishes and so he didn't have to do them. That's the crap I don't want to put up with anymore. I'm really excited about getting my own place for the first time."

## Balancing Family Responsibilities

Just like Darla and Maggie, Tim and Jessie developed a good relationship with their boomerang kid for the first time. Many other families that have always gotten along pretty well with their adult children also find that the reentry unexpectedly changes the existing family dynamics in a positive way. This is what happened when twenty-four-year-old Mike from Houston moved back home to save money.

Mike had graduated from college with a major in English literature, and soon found out that the world was not standing in line waiting to employ liberal arts graduates in high-paying entry-level jobs. After working for two years in the personnel department of an insurance company, Mike decided that what he really wanted to do was own and operate a bookstore. He began poring over college catalogues, and discovered that getting an M.B.A. would probably be a waste of money, but that General Accounting, Marketing, and Introduction to Business, all offered at the local community college, would give him what he needed. He also knew, after having been in the work force the past two years, that the most important thing he needed could never be found in a classroom. He needed firsthand experience working in a bookstore to learn all he could about the business before starting his own; but if he worked half time at a bookstore while he completed the necessary courses at the community college, he wouldn't be able to afford his present apartment. He approached his parents about moving back home for the year while he went to the community college.

Steve and Dorothy, Mike's parents, were in their early fifties. Their youngest child had just left home for college, and Dorothy was working full time for the first time since before her children were born. She was a salesperson in a small boutique and loved her job. When their son asked to move back home, Dorothy and Steve were pleased that he had such a well-thought-out plan and agreed to help. They got along well with Mike and didn't feel that his presence would be much of a problem. They didn't discuss any of the particulars of Mike's return, other than agreeing that he would live at home for the academic year. They all assumed that things would work out just fine because it was a mutual decision to have Mike move back home, and there certainly wasn't any kind of crisis involved.

In September, when Mike moved in, it was the first time he had lived at home in the six years since his senior year in high school. At first his relationship with his parents was pleasant and relaxed, but before long they all slipped back into old parent-child roles.

"I just threw my clothes down the clothes chute like I always had when I lived at home, and Mom started doing my laundry. It was a lot easier than doing it myself, so I figured I might as well let her," Mike told us. "Then she started yelling at me to clean my room and even telling me to get a haircut. I felt like I was in high school again, and I resented it. I stopped eating dinner at home so often, but Dad would get mad if I didn't call to tell them whether I'd be there or not."

Dorothy told us, "All of a sudden I realized that, just like Steve and Mike, I was working, and at a full-time job — only I fell back into being the wife and mother just as though I wasn't working outside the home. I was so tired. I was working all day, and still doing all the grocery shopping, the cooking, the dishes, and the laundry for these men. I found myself getting mad not only at Mike but at Steve, too."

The tension in the home and in Dorothy and Steve's own relationship forced everyone to sit down and seek a solution. "There wasn't a darn thing I could say when Dorothy pointed out how unfair the situation was," Steve said. "Change isn't that easy for me, and I had never been very domestic. I married Dorothy right after I got out of the army, and I had always had someone else to do the cooking, first my mother, then the army, then Dorothy. But now I knew I would have to do my share."

Dorothy added, "Now I look at the trouble we had when Mike first moved in as a blessing in disguise. I had been doing all the housework as well as working before he moved in, and it didn't seem odd to me; but with the addition of one more person, I felt burdened. Things have really changed around here. We split everything up three ways and take turns with the housework, and everyone does his or her own laundry."

"One thing I've really enjoyed is cooking with Dad," Mike said. "Since I was on my own for those two years, I've had to do a lot more of it than he has, and it's nice to be able to help show him something for a change. I feel like we are three adults living together, and we've had some great times and some good laughs. Mom really cracked up when Dad washed all his underwear with his red T-shirt and everything turned pink."

For this family, Mike's return served as a catalyst for a positive change in the way Dorothy and Steve related not only to Mike, but to one another.

## Moving Beyond Parent-Child Roles

All the families who found living with their boomerang kid a good experience were able to move beyond their old parent-child roles. Many of them had to make a conscious effort to form new relationships. One mother who had two teenagers still living with her when her twenty-five-year-old daughter boomeranged home said, "I had to deliberately relate to Carolyn differently because she was an adult and it wasn't right for me to treat her the way I did the younger kids. Whenever I found myself wanting to say something about her clothes, her hair, how she spent her time, the state of her room, or any of the kinds of things I used to say as a mother, I asked myself if I would tell another adult, a friend of mine who might be staying with me, to come home by midnight or suggest what dress she might wear. It put things in perspective quickly and helped me to keep my mouth shut."

As this mother found, a changed relationship doesn't happen automatically; countless parents told us they had to remind themselves repeatedly not to interfere in matters of their young adult's life where they knew they didn't belong. A father of a twenty-four-year-old son who moved back home after losing his job said, "One of the hardest things for me to accept was that my son had to make his own mistakes; that, in fact, it would be the only way he'd really learn. Once that dawned on me, I began to let go. Everything got easier between us, and I felt free to actually enjoy him."

The mother of a twenty-three-year-old boomerang kid told us, "It was terribly hard at first when my daughter moved back home: her finances were in a mess, she was depressed about a love affair that hadn't worked out, and she had just quit a job she hated, with no idea of what to do next. Her father and I agreed that while she was trying to find a more satisfying job she needed to master skills for living on her own, so in exchange for room and board she became our family bookkeeper. It wasn't just a kid-type job doing chores like walking the dog or taking out the trash. She had to take over making our bank deposits, paying our monthly bills, keeping records for taxes — I think before this experience she thought we had this endless supply of money that magically never ran out. This gave her a chance to see that there isn't any magic, that budgeting and planning is the same process no matter what the level of income and expenses is, and that her father and I had to exercise control and discipline, set limits on our spending, and save to meet certain goals. The most rewarding thing for us as parents was watching Barbara change and grow during the year she lived with us. She felt hopeless and defeated when she first moved in, but by the end of the year she was a more confident young woman and had acquired a solid practical view of the world, eager to make her way in it. Watching her grow, seeing her become stronger and more self-sufficient, gave us such pleasure. We had really helped her."

Another family told us that they didn't know how they would have managed if their twenty-five-year-old son hadn't moved back with them. Kathleen, a New York woman in her early fifties, said, "Our son Tyler had his two room-mates take off leaving him holding the bag on the rent while he was in graduate school. We had to bail him out, and he came home to live for the rest of the semester. Right after he moved in, my eighty-year-old mother fell and broke her hip. She came to live with us, and Tyler and my husband and I all pitched in to care for her. I can't tell you how wonderful it was to have another adult around. It gave my husband and me a break so we could occasionally get away and have some time to ourselves. The family was cemented in a way it hadn't been before; and the three of us, my husband, my son, and I, were a team, a team of adults."

But the rejoicing didn't all come from the parents. Young adults, too, talked about their second chance to grow up and to be closer to their parents. For some, the opportunity to resolve conflicts from the past eased their passage to maturity. A twenty-three-year-old San Diego woman said, "My parents were divorced when I was nine, and my dad moved away to L.A. I stayed in San Diego and lived with my mom — after he moved I only saw Dad a few times a year. After I graduated from college, I traveled for a year and then moved in with Mom while I was job hunting. I lived with her for a year while I was saving money to move out. While I was away at college, my dad had moved back to San Diego; the year I lived with Mom was the first time I had lived in the same city with him since I was nine. I thought it would be a chance for us to really get to know each other. But it turned out to be a hard year; I kept hoping that he could find time for me and would want to see me and get to know me, but I didn't see any more of him than I had when he lived in L.A. It hurt a lot. I realized that I had always made excuses for him, telling myself that he and I didn't have much of a relationship because he lived in a different city. But this time I had to face who he was and realize that I never was going to get him to be the father I wanted. It was a sad time; sometimes I felt almost as though someone had died. But it was my wish for a dad that was dying. As hard as it was, I was glad I had that year to face it — with Mom to help me. The whole thing of my wishing I had a father I could be close to finally felt resolved. When I moved out, I felt like I really could get on with my life and with being an adult."

Over and over again we saw that the families that adapted well to the return of their young adult son or daughter did not dodge the financial aspects of the situation. The young adults paid rent or contributed in some concrete way to the household, thus averting resentment on the part of parents and creating an atmosphere where the young adult felt more like a true adult pulling his or her own weight.

The sentiments we heard were echoed in a *New York Times* article that quoted a young woman living with her parents as saying, "You get to see your parents in a different light. It really is a wonderful time, a transition period that wasn't available before. Ten or 15 years ago people married to get out of the house, but now we have more choices."[1]

The transitional time when the young adult boomerangs home offers a time to heal and repair troubled relationships from the past, a time when the young adult learns to say good-bye to childhood, and a time for the parents to say good-bye to their past mistakes. As parents master the difficult task of letting go, they open the door for their adult child's friendship and love, and experience the quiet joy that comes from witnessing the strengthening of an evolving young human spirit.

# EIGHT

## Leaving Is Easier the Second Time Around

### *Knowing When It's Time to Let Go*

WHAT SIGNALS Punxsutawney Phil to emerge from his hole on February 2? What summons the swallows back to San Juan Capistrano annually on March 19? And when is it time for the boomerang kid to move back out into the world? In all of these situations, something inside, something outside.

Striving toward independence begins very early in human beings. Somewhere around the fifth month, infants begin crawling and putting things into their mouths, pushing themselves into a larger world, to gain more mastery of it. Freud remarked that all children's play is dominated by the wish to be grown-up and to be able to do what grown-ups do; we can see that every day as we watch children playing house, store, doctor, or school, arguing about who gets to be the grown-up. There is, deep inside all human beings, a wish to be in control of one's own life, to be as free of as many external and internal restraints as possible. Most of the young adults who have returned home for a period of time will begin to feel the urge once again to be independent and free of the constraints of living with their parents. Just as the psychological separation of the infant from its parents gradually takes place from the fifth month to the thirty-sixth month of life, so the returning young adult will need a period of time to gain the skills needed for successful independent living. Some babies walk at nine months, while others struggle to their feet well after their first birthday. Some young adults will adapt quickly to becoming fully functioning adult members of the household and master without too much struggle the skills they need to make their way in the world as independent people; others will move at a slower pace. As parents, we need to allow for that "different drummer" in each young adult.

In most cases young adults move home to get back on their feet, either financially or emotionally or both. Their job is to learn the skills that will enable them to handle their lives on their own again. Their parents' job is to help them achieve that goal by having appropriate expectations of them while honoring their autonomy.

## Has Your Adult Child Kept the Agreements?

A good yardstick against which to measure a young person's readiness to leave is to look at the way he or she has handled the agreements you made about living at home. Has your adult child generally lived up to his or her part of the bargain? Look at not just *whether* the agreements have been kept, but the *way* in which they've been kept. One young woman came home so fearful and anxious about the way she had wrecked her life by using cocaine that for months she would continually check in with her parents for a weather report on her progress: "How'm I doing, Mom?" and "Do you think I'm handling things okay, Dad?" Although she'd been free of cocaine, she wasn't ready to leave until she no longer needed constant reassurance from her parents.

As young children develop, they gradually move beyond

obeying parents because of fear of parental disapproval; accepting limits becomes a part of their own internal code. Young adults leaving home need to be beyond the stage of needing continual reminders or reassurance. They should be keeping their agreements easily and routinely, not to avoid punishment or gain approval, but because keeping agreements is a part of adult makeup, part of an internal code. They keep agreements with their parents *because they said they would.*

Has keeping promises now become a part of the way your young adult sees him- or herself, a part of personal integrity? Some parents use the original contract they made as a checklist, not in the same rigid and precise way that a pilot must check off every item on the preflight list before the plane can fly, but in order to ask, did the young adult generally keep his or her part of the bargain? Did he or she learn to handle finances by paying bills on time, budgeting money to meet expenses, paying back loans from you, keeping records of money spent and resisting impulses to buy things that really weren't affordable? Was he or she able to save enough to move out and also have a financial safety net?

How about the household: did he or she behave as a fully contributing adult member? Share responsibility for household tasks? Do what he or she agreed to reasonably well, and on time? Take initiative in finding jobs that needed to be done, without being asked? Was he or she thoughtful and considerate toward others in the household most of the time?

In regard to the particular problems that brought your adult child home, has he or she now thought about different ways to approach these areas? Is he or she less impulsive and more thoughtful about important decisions? Able to see the consequences of his or her actions and to reason, "If I do this, then this will happen and that will lead to . . ."?

In general, does your boomerang kid act like an adult or still seem like an adolescent?

## Indications That Adolescence Is Over

The use of the word *adolescent* dates back to 1430 when it was used to describe the years fourteen to twenty-five in males, twelve to twenty-one in females; it means, literally, "becoming an adult." Peter Blos, a psychoanalyst specializing in adolescence, proposes a terminal stage of adolescence, late to postadolescence, which is really preadult life.[1] While there are some arbitrary limits about the ending of adolescence (some say eighteen, some argue twenty-two, others say all the way to twenty-nine), a better way to define the ending of this tumultuous period is to look for psychological closure or the successful completion of some important challenges necessary to take on an adult life. Although they are not hard-and-fast rules regarding a boomerang kid's readiness to leave, the following psychological barometers can provide useful indications:

1. Have the mood swings of adolescence, the highs and lows, leveled out? Do the young adults have the ability to keep their emotions to themselves when appropriate? Do they have the ability to select which feelings they will share only with intimates and which with those not so close to them? Are they discriminating as far as where and when they reveal these feelings? Do they recognize a full range of emotional responses inside themselves?

2. Are they less impulsive? Can their behavior be predicted with some degree of accuracy — that is, do they tend usually to behave the same way in the same circumstances? Do they have more self-understanding, with a decreasing need always to be understood by others? Are they more certain, less tentative, about decisions?

Are they more reasoned, and less arbitrary and rebellious in their opinions?

3. Do they have a life-style beginning to take shape that seems to be based on a realistic sense of the options and alternatives they can explore? Have they set reasonable goals to work toward? Do they have an inner sense of where they are going and who they will be when they get there? Do they show motivation to achieve their goals and attain the life-style they want through their own efforts?

4. Has the young adults' struggle seemed to move from inside to outside, from being self-involved to being able to take others into account? Are they enjoying friendships based on shared values and ideas, perhaps becoming active in group activities that focus on particular interests? As they look for their place in society, do they have a better understanding of how changes are brought about, and feel they can make a difference as part of a group?

5. Do they have a solid sense of sexual identity? Do they understand what it means to be a man or a woman in today's society and know that their security in their role comes from inside themselves and not from old, reassuring but limited symbols such as the cars and clothes they may have surrounded themselves with in adolescence? Is there a shift away from indiscriminate personal and social relationships toward more careful involvements and eventual commitments? Despite the natural upheavals in human relationships, can they sustain close ties with friends and acquaintances?

6. Have they tried, in both their thinking and their behavior, not to let the emotional hurts of childhood keep them from having an adult-to-adult relationship with parents? Can they now accept responsibility for the

person they are today, forgiving their parents for who they are, for what they did or didn't do?[2,3]

## Don't Expect Perfection

These objective measures all sound pretty reasonable, but in reality no one ever gets it all *that* together. Beware of the myth that, after their time at home, mature post-adolescent young adults will always be able to conduct their lives in a completely orderly, planned, healthy manner, responding to all the expected environmental stresses in life (illness, death, divorce, changes in employment, relationship losses, and so on) with successful solutions and good humor. No adult, young or old, manages that every time! Crises occur in everyone's life; they may be the kind that knock the socks off or barely ruffle the hair. The capacity to deal with the various crises in life depends on an individual's resources, past experiences, and the ability to think under pressure, as well as a level of trust that lets him or her ask for and accept help.

## The Difficulty of Letting Go

We titled this chapter "Leaving Is Easier the Second Time Around." But while it may be *easier,* leaving is never *easy,* whether it's the first time, or the third or fourth or fifth. And for the parents of young adults leaving home, the challenge of letting go is a great one. In the first place, someone you love very much is leaving you. Second, your son or daughter is now reasonably capable of making it on his or her own, without you. You're not needed anymore. Even though enhancing the competency of this young person is what the whole process has been about, it still hurts not to be needed. Dr. Helene Deutsch has commented that

> every phase of a child's development ends with intensified tendencies to liberate himself. The mother, every mother, tries to keep him attached to herself and opposes the actions that tend to dissolve the tie. Maternal overprotection, in its numerous forms and variations, serves the purpose of preserving the child's dependence and averting the separation trauma for the mother. The most direct means to this end is infantilization, that is, the attempt to keep the child childishly helpless as long as possible. The over-indulgent as well as the domineering mother leads to the same end, that is the dependence of the child.[4]

Parents, especially mothers, struggle against a deep force inside them that drives them to keep the young adult dependent. Besides the sadness involved in giving up having this young adult around, you have to give up the gratification you get as caretaker of someone in a dependent position.

And, as if that weren't enough, you may have another, often surprising, seemingly conflicting emotion to deal with: jealousy. Young adults usually have far more options than their parents did (this is especially true for daughters), and both sons and daughters are usually better educated and more psychologically prepared to take advantage of the possibilities the world offers. You may criticize your daughter for asking a man with whom she works to have dinner with her, and not recognize that the feeling behind the criticism is really envy of the freedom she enjoys. You may find yourself critical of your son's indecision about several job offers he has received, and not perceive your underlying envy of his many choices. Recognizing your envy is the first step toward dealing with what is a natural response to watching your adult child have so much more opportunity than you had. Accepting that youth has many qualities worthy of envy, you can move away from criticism and begin to express the support and enthusiasm your adult child needs from you.

For you as parents, watching your children move ahead with their lives may stimulate a return of all the fantasies of your own youth. You may wish there had been more sexual freedom and more educational or career opportunities when you'd been starting out on your own. You may feel threatened and saddened as you realize that what lies ahead for a son or daughter is in the past for you; your own remaining options can seem, by comparison, few and limited. You have already chosen your life's work, and if you find it less than satisfying you may feel locked into it. For some parents, marriage may seem stale and uninteresting, and the partner chosen in youth unsatisfying now; but finding someone new may seem impossible. The rose-colored glasses came off years ago, often to be replaced with gray- or blue-tinted ones.

We sometimes overlook that parents, too, have their own struggles: to mourn for their lost youth, and to grieve for all the lost options. Even in the best of marriages, those where the couple has remained deeply in love, this grieving takes place. It is a natural process that helps you let go of the past, close the chapter on the child-raising years, and prepare to enjoy the years to come. Some depression is normal, and you'll get through it. It's best to allow yourself to feel the loss; sometimes the inability or failure to mourn can lead to a midlife depression and a continued sense of dissatisfaction. In addition, we have found that when parents do not recognize some of their own feelings of depression and envy of the adult son or daughter, they will often express these feelings as criticism of the young adult and deny the young adult's readiness to go.

## *Other Reasons Parents Hang On*

The boomerang period, for all its hassles, may have been a relatively happy time for the family; and the loss of this satisfaction of helping your children get back on their feet creates a void in your life that you will have to fill in some other way now. The empty nest brings the marital relationship into focus, and sometimes that relationship seems as empty as the nest. A national poll reported in the *Seattle Times* found that couples talk to each other, really talk with each other about themselves, about seventeen minutes per week. This is a startling figure that works out to about an hour a month — less time than most people spend switching channels on the television set, watering the plants, or opening the mail. It's no wonder some parents have a hard time with their own relationship when the kids finally leave home. Often the conflicts they have had in the marriage have been acted out in a triangle with the children; and with the removal of this third corner of the family system, some parents must face the fact that their fight and disappointment may be with each other. Often their dependent adult children have met the parents' needs for the companionship and comfort that they have been unable to find with each other. When this young adult companion leaves for his or her own life, the parents are forced to look for a new balance in the marriage without the gratification of dependent children, a balance that includes meeting each other's needs and wishes for companionship, emotional support, and sexual satisfaction.

Sometimes parents contribute to and prolong the dependency of their adult children in order to avoid facing the emptiness of their marital relationship. Middle-aged couples with a revolving door on the family home, through which their adult children are continually boomeranging in and out, are often trying to ward off having to face a dying marriage. In turn, boomerang kids find it harder to leave these parents, not only because they have been seduced by a comfortable life-style with low expectations, but also because they feel responsible and obligated to keep their parents' marriage together. To stay avoids painful guilt.

Single parents, whether widowed or divorced, and their young adult children often struggle mutually with letting go of each other. Dr. Helene Deutsch has said, "Many mothers in their attempt to tie their children to themselves appeal cleverly and consistently to guilty feelings: 'You will abandon me, who has suffered so much.' "[5] The boomerang kid may respond to this often unconscious communication with an overdeveloped concern for the single parent's welfare, feeling too guilty to leave.

## Abandonment Guilt

This kind of guilt has a powerful pull, different from what we feel when we break our internal codes of right and wrong or don't live up to our ideals in an internally acceptable way. It is the guilt a mother feels leaving her infant for the first time with a sitter, or her youngster on his or her first day of school; it is the guilt a boomerang kid may feel when leaving a parent who has become dependent on him or her during this time of living at home. It is best termed abandonment guilt. Such feelings arise when we come to see someone as incomplete, as needing us in some desperate way. The pain we feel for our part of the hurt, the leaving, makes the separating harder.

You are responding to this feeling when you first allow your adult child to return home, for to refuse would feel like abandoning him or her in a time of need. You may have to deal with this guilt again when it is time to let the adult child go, especially if you are unsure your young adult is ready to handle responsibility. You may feel as if you are abandoning this unfinished human being out in the cold world. In the same way, the young adult who is having a difficult time leaving the parent he or she has been living with may be struggling with some inappropriate sense of responsibility for that parent's life.

If you find yourself caught in this web, remind yourself of your and your adult child's individual autonomy — that each of you is in charge of your own life. Just as it's not your job to ensure your adult child's happiness, it is not his or her job to "fix" your marriage or provide a life for you as a single parent. Facing an unhappy marriage isn't easy, nor is it easy to carve out a satisfying life as a middle-aged single person; but that job belongs to you. You, not your children, are responsible for your happiness. Many middle-aged single parents find therapy helpful when their adult children leave, and we know of many couples who have used marital counseling at this time to rebuild a life together. The leaving of adult children is another major milestone and an important time to learn to do something new, to relate to each other in a new way.

## Accepting Your Adult Child's Limitations

Sometimes our children disappoint us; sometimes we wish they had turned out differently. And that is another loss. One mother told us about her daughter who had lived at home for six months after the breakup of a relationship. "Joan is a wonderful young woman. I know lots of mothers brag about their kids, but she really is exceptionally talented and capable. She has lots of good friends and a great job as personnel director at a large computer company. Joan lived with us after she broke up with Ben and, although she was terribly sad for a while, it didn't take her that long to start dating again. Now she thinks she's in love again and she's getting ready to move in with this new man. If I try to talk to her about her relationships, she gets furious with me for interfering. But I see her repeating the same pattern over and over. She always picks these very dependent, needy men where she can dominate the relationship. She doesn't have enough self-esteem to pick someone who really could be her equal. I know that in spite of all her achievements, deep down Joan is an anxious little kid. She can't be without a man, and she picks the kind that won't leave her. I feel so disappointed for her, and I feel so disappointed in myself. Because I feel that somewhere along the way it must have been my fault that Joan is so anxious and fearful of being alone."

Working through this kind of disappointment requires learning to accept our children as they are, and accepting the mistakes we made that may have contributed to the problems they struggle with. It helps to remember that they still are young adults with years ahead of them to develop and grow. Joan at twenty-five may be capable only of a dependent and limited relationship with a man, but Joan at forty may be quite a different story. Patience is not a virtue intrinsic to Western cultures or valued by contemporary American society; we tend to want quick solutions and easy answers. Americans are apt to interpret patience as passivity. It's important to remember, however, that things take time. Don't write these kids off. As their lives unfold, they will grow and change.

## Anger and the Leaving Process

Often, right before your boomerang kid leaves, everything may seem to crumble. You'll fight. You'll start being irritated about all sorts of trivial things that at any other time probably wouldn't matter that much. Your adult child will yell at you, "Quit treating me like I'm two!" and you'll

yell back, "I would if you'd stop acting like a baby!" You'll
think everything is a failure and you're back to square one.
What happened?

There's an old saying that it's better to be mad than sad.
People who love each other *are* sad when they have to leave
each other. And these are two sides of the same coin: one
is leaving, the other is being left. Often, to avoid that sadness, families fight. Don't worry, the fights are usually not
a big deal, and when the leaving is over, you can go back
to being good friends again. You just need some fighting
right now to help you distance and disengage from each
other. It's the little push needed to get the kid out of the
nest, and you back in it where you belong.

Once we're able to wrench ourselves away from that
primitive urge to hang on to our children, a very special
relationship develops to fill the void. We can become friends,
adult friends. This is probably as good a place as any to
remind ourselves that in many ways our children are really
so much more than just our children. As Kahlil Gibran
wrote in *The Prophet*:

> *Your children are not your children.*
> *They are the sons and daughters of Life's longing for itself.*
> *They come through you but not from you,*
> *And though they are with you yet they belong not to you.*
> *You may give them your love but not your thoughts,*
> *For they have their own thoughts.*
> *You may house their bodies but not their souls,*
> *For their souls dwell in the house of tomorrow,*
> *Which you cannot visit, even in your dreams.*
> *You may strive to be like them, but seek not to make them*
> *like you.*
> *For life goes not backward nor tarries with yesterday.*
> *You are the bows from which your children as living arrows*
> *are sent forth.*

When we have a broken arm, we have a cast put on it. When the bone heals, we have the cast taken off. None of us would think of wearing the cast for a lifetime. When the hurt that the boomerang kid comes home to recover from has healed, we need to withdraw the support system he or she needed during the mending process. With the ending of "childhood" once again, the young adult and his or her parents are faced with yet more changes and challenges. This is a time of balanced joy and sadness: joy that there was a time of renewal and repair, closeness yet separateness; sadness that once again our lives will go in different directions and begin without each other. While we are parents forever, our parenting role is not perpetual. In his meditation on life's cycles, T. S. Eliot could have been writing about this particular time in the lives of parents and young adult children when he said, "To make an end is to make a beginning."

# Notes

INTRODUCTION

1. Frank Conroy, "America in a Trance," *Esquire* (1968; reprinted in *Esquire,* June 1983), p. 115.
2. Gloria Steinem, "The Moral Disarmament of Betty Coed," *Esquire* (1962; reprinted in *Esquire,* June 1983), p. 243.
3. Rep. Jim Wright, " 'You Can Have It All,' Nifty Slogan, Sad Myth," *Rocky Mountain News* (February 10, 1986).
4. Thomas J. Moore, "Legions of 'New Poor' Continue Hungry Slide Into Poverty," *Seattle Times* (February 2, 1986).
5. Srully Blotnick, "Why Hippies Beget Yuppies," *Forbes* (February 24, 1986), p. 146.
6. "Suicide Part I," *Harvard Medical School Mental Health Letter* 2:8 (February 1986), p. 1.

CHAPTER TWO

1. George E. Vaillant, *Adaptation to Life* (Boston: Little, Brown, 1977), p. 215.
2. Margaret S. Mahler, M.D., *The Selected Papers of Margaret S. Mahler, M.D., Vol. II, Separation-Individuation* (New York: Jason Aronson, 1979), p. 120.
3. Vaillant, pp. 203, 210.
4. Ibid., p. 216.
5. Garrison Keillor, "Storm Home," *News of Lake Wobegon: Winter* (St. Paul: Minnesota Public Radio, 1983), side two (audio tape).

6. Susan Littwin, *The Postponed Generation: Why America's Kids Are Growing Up Later* (New York: Morrow, 1986), p. 15.

CHAPTER SIX

1. Winifred Gallagher, "The Dark Affliction of Mind and Body," *Discover* (May 1986), p. 67.
2. Ibid.
3. Silvano Arieti, M.D., *Understanding and Helping the Schizophrenic: A Guide for Family and Friends* (New York: Simon and Schuster, 1979), p. 14.
4. Harold M. Schmeck, Jr., "Advancing on Schizophrenia," *New York Times* (March 18, 1986).
5. Arieti, p. 170.
6. "Cocaine Abuse," *Harvard Medical School Mental Health Letter* 2:5 (November 1985), p. 2.

CHAPTER SEVEN

1. Robert Lindsey, "A New Generation Finds It Hard to Leave the Nest," *New York Times* (January 15, 1984).

CHAPTER EIGHT

1. Peter Blos, *The Adolescent Passage* (New York: International Universities Press, 1979), p. 63.
2. Ibid., p. 76.
3. ———, "When and How Does Adolescence End: Structural Criteria for Adolescent Closure," *Adolescent Psychiatry: Developmental and Clinical Studies,* edited by Sherman Feinstein and Peter Giovacchini (New York: Jason Aronson, 1977), Vol. I, p. 5.
4. Helene Deutsch, *The Psychology of Women* (New York: Grune and Stratton, 1945), Vol. II, p. 158.
5. Ibid.